HARD TRAVELING

Carlos Arnaldo Schwantes

Hard Traveling

A Portrait of Work Life in the New Northwest

UNIVERSITY OF NEBRASKA PRESS

LINCOLN AND LONDON

Library of Congress
Cataloging in Publication Data
Schwantes, Carlos A., 1945–
Hard traveling: a portrait of work
life in the New North-
west / Carlos Arnaldo Schwantes.
p. cm.   Includes bib-
liographical references and index.
ISBN 0-8032-4221-2
1. Migrant labor – Northwest, Pacific – History. 2. Blue col-
lar workers – Northwest Pacific –
History. 1. Title.
HD5856.U5S34 1995
331.5′44′09795 – dc20 94-160
CIP

Dedicated to My Grandparents:

Arnaldo Pedro Schwantes and
Estanislava Laura Goreczna.

Charles Henry Casteen and
Ruth Frances Smith.

Three Continents, One Faith.

Contents

1. Two loggers pose on springboards or planks anchored in the tree trunk. This western innovation for felling trees saved clearing underbrush, avoided large pockets of pitch, and made cutting through the oversize bases of species like Sitka spruce and Douglas fir unnecessary. Until the 1880s, fallers chopped down the trees, and buckers cut or "bucked" them into standard lengths with crosscut saws commonly called Swede fiddles or misery whips. When loggers in the California redwoods discovered that they could use saws to fall trees, the new technique spread quickly up the coast. In 1909, shortly after Washington emerged as the nation's number one lumber-producing state (in terms of product value), 63 percent of its wageworkers in manufacturing depended upon the lumber industry for jobs. The number remained well above 50 percent for many years. By comparison, in 1909, Oregon, Idaho, and Montana ranked seventeenth, thirty-second, and thirty-fifth respectively as lumber-producing states. At that time Washington, if not yet the rest of the New Northwest, could accurately be described as a "sawdust empire." Courtesy Historical Photograph Collections, Washington State University Libraries, Pratsch no. 435.

In the West, especially, the long distances between industrial centers force upon migratory
workers the undesirable alternatives of spending their funds for traveling expenses, or of resorting to the freight cars. While spending the
summer at a point between Portland and
Spokane the writer has had opportunity to see
the freight trains pass, and passenger trains,
too, for that matter, with men stealing rides in
every conceivable place in and on the cars. In
talking with these men, as they would sometimes be put off by the trainmen, they all told
the same story of their attempt to reach the
harvest fields, where they hoped to find work.
Apparently, "our bumper crops" are gathered,
in part at least, by wandering, homeless men
who are forced to beg by the roadside bread
that comes from the grain they are eager to
harvest. – A. E. Wood exhibit, presented to the
U.S. Commission on Industrial Relations,
Portland, Oregon, August 1914

Commissioner O'Connell. What is the condition comparatively between the horses and human beings as to bunking arrangements?
Mr. Brown. Well, the beds are always made for
the horses, the other fellows have to make
their own beds, if they are made. Usually these
men are tired out, and have no chance to, or
care or desire to improve their conditions.
They just come in and sleep. Nearly all of these
camps are infested with bedbugs, some of
them have fleas, and some of them are lousy.
One camp down on Grays Harbor – the men
last summer went out and slept out doors in
the woods, rather than tolerate the conditions
in the bunk house. They would take their bed
and go out and sleep on the ground in the
woods. They did that for quite a period of time
to get rid of the bed bugs. – Testimony of J. G.
Brown, describing living conditions in logging
camps, before U.S. Commission on Industrial
Relations, Seattle, Washington, August 1914

2. Brawny warehouse workers in the McConnell Grain Warehouse in Pullman, Washington, pose with a large sack of oats circa 1895. Until the late 1920s, virtually all wheat from the interior Northwest traveled to distant markets in sacks, each one sewn shut by hand. This labor-intensive process developed, in part, because grain had to be handled so many times as it traveled from fields, down the Snake and Columbia rivers via steamboats and portage railroads to the docks of Portland. There it was loaded aboard oceangoing ships for markets as distant as England. Not until World War II made burlap sacks prohibitively expensive was the transition to modern methods of bulk shipment completed. Courtesy Historical Photograph Collections, Washington State University Libraries, no.79-005.

Preface

Most illustrations in this book depict work life in Oregon, Washington, Idaho, and Montana in the late nineteenth and early twentieth centuries. Collectively they make visible what general histories of the West have until recently often failed to notice or fully comprehend: the existence of an informal commonwealth of toil that at various times encompassed not just these four states but also major portions of the entire West.[1] Pioneer photographers preserved on film many views of work life in California, Arizona, Utah, and elsewhere, but my purpose here is not simply to compile a picture album. I seek instead to use historical photographs to portray the people and events most often associated with work in the West and especially to examine how photographers themselves shaped popular perceptions of labor. For such purposes it seems appropriate to concentrate on the Pacific Northwest, the part of the West already most familiar to me, and on those features of work life that did most to define the region during the years of supercharged development and change from the 1880s through the 1920s.

During these four critical decades the part of work life in the New Northwest that generated the most comment was the "hard traveling" demanded of a veritable army of manual laborers who worked in the forests, fields, and mines — in the three industries that together with fisheries on the Pacific Coast dominated the regional economy. The term, immortalized in Woody Guthrie's song "Hard Travelin'," offers an apt summary of the subject of this book. In the subtitle and throughout the text I have used the term *New Northwest* to emphasize that the Pacific Northwest during the turn-of-the-century era was in so many important ways lit-

erally created anew. Commentators have used the term also to avoid confusing the new and rapidly evolving states in the nation's Far Corner with the Great Lakes states of the *old* Northwest Territory.

Seven of the eight folios of images that constitute the second portion of *Hard Traveling* highlight important aspects of work life in the New Northwest during the years of rapid transformation. The eighth folio focuses on depression and war during the 1930s and 1940s, although the post-1930s era, when older modes of work life had largely disappeared as a defining element in the region's labor history, is not a primary concern of this book. Arranged to complement the photographic record are firsthand observations by or about wage earners, such as are contained in the guides to each of the four Northwest states prepared by the Federal Writers' Project of the Works Progress Administration. Also of value are statements from the United States Commission on Immigration and Richard Neuberger's evocative comments on life in the 1930s contained in *Our Promised Land*.[2]

Some of the most trenchant comments on manual labor in the Pacific Northwest come from the United States Commission on Industrial Relations, which during the summer of 1914 held hearings in Butte, Seattle, and Portland to probe working conditions in the nation's Far Corner. Congress established this organization in 1912 to investigate the increasing industrial violence that characterized labor-management relations in the United States. Among the members appointed by President Woodrow Wilson were John B. Lennon, American Federation of Labor treasurer, James O'Connell, head of the International Association of Machinists, Austin Bruce Garretson, choice of the railway brotherhoods, and John R. Commons, professor at the University of Wisconsin and longtime student of labor relations in the United States. "The nine members of the Industrial Relations Commission," declared the journalist Walter Lippmann, "have before them the task of explaining why America, supposed to become the land of promise, has become the land of disappointment and deep-seated discontent."[3]

In searching for images of western work life I received various forms of help that now deserve to be acknowledged. The John Calhoun Smith Memorial Fund underwrote most of the cost of travel and research for *Hard Traveling;* its continued support has been a welcome, even vital, part of my professional life at the University of Idaho. The history chair Kent Hackmann deserves special thanks for his vigorous promotion of research and writing within the department, as do also Evelyne Pickett and Nancy Dafoe for their help at critical times. Offering their own special forms of encouragement were Kurt O. Olsson, dean of the College of Letters and Science; Thomas O. Bell, provost, and Elisabeth Zinser, president of the University of Idaho.

Many individuals took time to guide me through their often voluminous collections of photographs and other documents. I am especially indebted to Terry Abraham, head of special collections at the University of Idaho; Edward Nolan, formerly of the Eastern Washington State Historical Society in Spokane and now with the Washington State Historical Society in Tacoma; Richard Engeman of the University of Washington's Pacific Northwest Collection; W. Thomas White of the James Jerome Hill Reference Library, Saint Paul; Susan Seyl of the Oregon Historical Society, Portland; and Elizabeth Jacox of the Idaho State Historical Society, Boise. Thanks go also to Walter Nugent of the University of Notre Dame for helping me to develop the concept of a wageworkers' frontier in his 1984 National Endowment for the Humanities Summer Seminar at Indiana University, and to Richard Maxwell Brown for his 1980 National Endowment for the Humanities Summer Seminar at the University of Oregon. *Hard Traveling* is only one of several of my books to have derived from those two seminars. William G. Robbins of the history department at Oregon State University took time from his own busy schedule to offer me numerous suggestions for improving the manuscript. I alone am responsible for any errors or omissions that may occur on the following pages.

The New Northwest as Wageworkers' Frontier

Our State is unfortunate in having so much seasonal work. Our heavy fruit production, which is gaining rapidly, requires employees for a relatively limited part of the year. The cultivation period and winter months need few persons compared to the short period when fruit is being picked and packed. This means that much of the help absolutely required in the fruit season must seek other work or is thrown into idleness during the remainder of the year. Logging operations also have periods, the exceedingly dry weather or worst months of winter usually seeing the camps closed down. Of the 45,502 farms of Oregon in 1910 it may be said that there is a heavy seasonal demand for labor, the peak load of course being reached in harvest days of late summer and fall. We have not, on the other hand, a very large percentage of industries requiring employees the year through as is found in the large eastern industrial centers. – The A. H. Averill Exhibit presented to the United States Commission on Industrial Relations, Portland, Oregon, August 1914.

In the East, with railroads closer together and trains more frequent, it is no calamity to a hobo to be "ditched" from a train. He usually could eat in the surrounding populated country, and all he had to do was wait an hour or two until the next train came along, or maybe he would just hop over to some other road and catch a train. The railroad bulls and train crews bothered him little, the Eastern hobo riding openly on the trains.

But in the sparsely populated West it was quite a different matter. Through the wide deserts and mountains the railroads were few and trains ran seldom. Hence a hobo ditched off a train might have to stick around a day or two waiting for another, probably with nothing to eat while doing so. And of course, in those days automobile roads were practically unknown in the West and hitch-hiking was still a thing of the future. – From William Z. Foster, *Pages from a Worker's Life* (1939), p.106

3. Construction of the St. Paul, Minneapolis & Manitoba Railroad across Montana Territory in 1887. Six years later, as the Great Northern Railway, it joined Saint Paul and Puget Sound to open a vast expanse of the New Northwest to settlement. One worker who helped build the Great Northern recalled with a measure of pride: "The track ahead was but a thin stripe upon the earth's white expanse. And upon this band of steel the hundred men, like animated tumbleweeds, bent and twisted, bored and scratched. Upon the white bosom of American earth we engraved a necklace of steel – set in tie plates, clasped with bolts and angle bars, brocaded with spikes. And there it lay secured to the earth, immovable." Stoyan Christowe, *My American Pilgrimage* (Boston: Little, Brown and Company, 1947). Courtesy Minnesota Historical Society, no. 2096.

4. L. A. Huffman photographed Northern Pacific tracklayers near Miles City, Montana, in 1881. Two years later at Gold Creek they completed the first northern transcontinental railroad to link the Great Lakes and Pacific Ocean. Courtesy Montana Historical Society, no. 981-370.

Portrait of Work Life

CHAPTER 1

In the Northwest everything seems to have happened within the last ten years; events which would be of epoch-making importance in any country at any time have here crowded one upon another with wanton prodigality, so that the Northwesterner, plumped down in the whirl of great things, can himself hardly grasp their full significance, contenting himself with confused superlatives. – Ray Stannard Baker, "The Great Northwest" (1903)

In a hitherto isolated valley located approximately sixty miles west of Helena, Montana Territory, near the confluence of the Clark Fork River and Gold Creek, two rival teams of railway construction workers raced one another to lay a final twelve hundred feet of track. Although the ends of the line had already met a few days earlier, this section was taken up to be spiked down a second time in a public display of joining East and West. After about twelve minutes of furious work, only one spike remained to complete the union. Several hundred onlookers crowded around the dignitaries who took turns hammering it home. The final spike and sledgehammer were specially wired so as to telegraph each blow to Northern Pacific Railroad officials waiting in Portland, Saint Paul, and New York. Their receivers recorded a last click at 5:18 P.M., signaling that the first northern transcontinental railroad was at last a reality.[1]

Saturday, September 8, 1883, was a day rich in symbolism for residents of the Pacific Northwest. At remote Gold Creek a newly erected wooden pavilion was decorated with pine boughs, bunting, and flags of Germany, Great Britain, and the United States. Capable of seating nearly a thousand people, it was filled with five trainloads of politicians, bankers, railroad officials, investors, journalists, and other special guests from North America and Europe who had assembled there as part of a lavish ceremony to celebrate completion of a railroad link that had been twenty years in the making. So slow and halting was the line's progress that many a Pacific Northwesterner had doubtless despaired of living long enough to see this day.

Alongside newly laid Northern Pacific track stood a sign that read "Lake Superior 1,198 miles / Puget Sound 847 miles." During the ceremony numerous dignitaries, including the former president Ulysses S. Grant, the former secretary of state William Evarts, and governors of the states and territories through which the railroad passed, dutifully trooped to the podium to extol the glory and importance of the Northern Pacific's achievement. Their elaborate orations lasted so long that the sun had disappeared behind the Montana hills before it was time to drive the final spike.

The festivities at Gold Creek proved a great promotional success for the Northern Pacific and signified the dawn of a new era for Pacific Northwesterners. The newness lay not in the railroad itself – local lines had existed in the region since the 1850s – but in the direct and convenient connection it provided to the East. Fourteen years after completion of the nation's first transcontinental railroad at Promontory, Utah, daily passenger trains commenced running between Saint Paul and Portland, with connecting service north to Tacoma. Less showy but even more vital were the freight trains that now threaded the canyons of the

5. Tacoma, "City of Destiny," juxtaposed to Mount Rainier, the Northwest's tallest peak, at the turn of the century. Tacoma, which became one of Washington's major industrial centers during the 1880s, was officially selected as the western terminus of the Northern Pacific Railroad in 1873. Ten years later when the line was completed, it provided newcomers easy access to the Pacific Northwest for the first time. As a result, the region experienced phenomenal growth.

During the 1880s alone, Washington's population increased by approximately 375 percent. Even more astounding was the growth of its cities, where population increases ranged from 1,000 percent in Seattle to 6,000 percent in Spokane. Industrial growth was no less rapid or spectacular. During the 1880s the value of Washington's industrial production increased by 1,100 percent. The supercharged pace of urban growth placed a premium on the skilled labor of carpenters, masons, plumbers, and other craftsmen, and so too did the great fires of 1889, which required rebuilding substantial portions of Seattle and Spokane. Courtesy Special Collections Division, University of Washington Libraries, Waite no.227-12.

6. Clarence Bisbee, a commercial photographer from Twin Falls, Idaho, strikes the expansive pose of a booster. Courtesy Idaho State Historical Society, no.73-221.1708.

Cascade Range and Rocky Mountains and steamed across the seemingly endless plains of eastern Montana.

Some of the day's symbolism was obvious, but some took the form of unintended irony, and none more so than the various types of juxtaposition that were clearly visible to the invited guests. Milling about the platform and reviewing stand were the financial barons of three nations, all in the accoutrements that symbolized power in America's Gilded Age, while huddled nearby in a small and somewhat sullen band were Crow Indians, dwellers of a shrinking hinterland who were doomed to experience great and lasting changes. During the previous summer, hunters had waited in vain for the great herds of buffalo that annually ranged south from Canada in search of food. Out of the millions of shaggy beasts that roamed the Great Plains only a decade earlier, fewer than two hundred remained in the entire American West the year of Gold Creek. During 1882 the Northern Pacific had hauled 200,000 hides out of Montana and Dakota.

The "iron wedding" also represented the juxtaposition of city and country. Gold Creek, like every western settlement along the railway corridor, found itself enmeshed in a vast new market economy created by the nation's expanding network of railway lines. Pacific Northwesterners would supply raw materials needed to fuel America's industrial expansion, while manufactured goods from the East and Midwest would flow west to stock the shelves of general stores and lumberyards in the nation's Far Corner. Many would call it a colonial relationship. Here too were the men who supplied the muscle power needed to build the new railway lines. They worked for wages, contrary to the popular impression that people went west to achieve personal freedom. For one moment the old West of Indians, trappers, and pioneers stood face to face with the new West of high finance, nationwide markets, and

rapid advances in communication and transportation. Wherever railroad tracks went, the old West confronted the new, but seldom so graphically as at Gold Creek.

The Northern Pacific line reduced to five or six days a tiresome journey that had once required several months of travel along the Oregon Trail. For investors and homeseekers from distant regions as well as for local residents, an era of isolation had ended. Two additional transcontinental railroads reached the region by 1893; but well before that date new cities and farms had transformed the Northwest landscape, and large-scale corporate enterprise and organized workers had attained unprecedented prominence and power. Largely as a result of the expanding infrastructure of railroad lines in the 1880s, the population of the Pacific Northwest increased from 322,000 to 907,000 during that decade alone, and that was only the beginning of forty years of extraordinary population growth and economic development.

The region experienced a brief period of hard times in the mid-1880s and a longer one from 1893 to 1897, but until the eve of the First World War the trend was toward more of everything positive, at least in the eyes of regional boosters. Tirelessly they compiled statistics documenting the growth of new cities like Portland, Seattle, and Spokane, the swelling output of the region's vital timber, fishing, and mining industries, and the expanding acreage of farmland in production. Doing most to promote the frenzied growth were the region's railroad companies, the largest of which served not merely as carriers of passengers and freight but also as transmitters of visual information to those who knew little about the nation's far Northwest. Ray Stannard Baker, a Pulitzer prize–winning journalist, grasped this fact early in the twentieth century when he naïvely suggested to a railroad agent that his company might be interested in development. "Why," responded the official, "the West is purely a railroad enterprise. We started it in our publicity department." The remark contained more than the usual grain of truth, thought Baker, who added that "the West was inevitable but the railroad was the instrument of its fate." Baker's comments underscored a major difference between development of the East or South and the West, which far more than the other two regions was a child of the railroad builders.[2]

Congress sought to spur construction of one transcontinental carrier, the Northern Pacific, by granting it a landed domain larger than the six New England states combined. The Northern Pacific together with its competitors the Union Pacific, the Southern Pacific, the Great Northern, and the Milwaukee Road issued hundreds of different promotional brochures from the 1870s through the 1920s, and even a few as late as the 1950s. Tens of thousands, possibly millions, of people scanned the various railroad tracts and broadsides that portrayed life in the Pacific Northwest essentially in terms of an advertiser's idealized civilization.

Boosters sought to inspire newcomers to find personal success and happiness in the natural landscape of a region that in the fevered prose of promoters often assumed the dimensions of nothing less than a "New Empire" of opportunity. If the Pacific Northwest came to connote anything during the decades of railroad promotion it was the superlative: "The gigantic forests, tremendous logging operations, sawmills, and paper mills; the titanic hydroelectric power plants, the stupendous irrigation projects – all typical of the vast scale of things in the Pacific Northwest are sights worth going to see," admonished one railroad wordsmith. Railroads amassed an incredible variety of statistics and photographs to tell the story of the New Empire in the Pacific Northwest and hired hundreds of agents to distribute the brochures throughout the East and northern Europe.[3]

To increase the appeal of their publications, railroads and other promoters purchased numerous "images of empire" from the region's commercial photographers. One of the most prominent of the camera artists in the late nineteenth century was F. Jay Haynes, the Northern Pacific's official photographer at Gold Creek. For thirty years, from 1876 to 1905, his images appeared frequently in railroad promotional literature. Haynes was typical of the region's commercial photographers who, apart from their portrait business, derived most of their income during the turn-of-the-century decades from the steady production of images that could be used to sell the Pacific Northwest.[4]

Some of the work of commercial photographers appeared on postcards and some was purchased by chambers of commerce, but their most important customers were the transcontinental railroads, which wanted photographs of bountiful crops, unsurpassed scenery, modern cities, and scenes of industry and technology to illustrate their promotional brochures. These publications sought to show how beautiful, modern, or progressive the Pacific Northwest was and, hence, why it was desirable as a home, place of business, tourist destination, and field for investment.

Recording the lives of workers who played a vital role in building the New Northwest was not ordinarily a part of the selling process. Heroic scenes from the logging industry were appropriate for a promotional brochure but certainly not photographs that showed ill-housed and unkempt migratory field hands or injury and death in the workplace. The region had no counterpart to Jacob Riis or Lewis Hine, whose documentary images of work life in the mills of the East provided a damning portrait of child labor and other abuses that

7. A promotional image used by the Chicago, Milwaukee & St. Paul Railway. Asahel Curtis photographed this harvest scene near Rosalia, Washington, in 1912. Courtesy Washington State Historical Society, A. Curtis no. 28660.

aided the cause of Progressive era reformers. The Danish-born Riis took his camera into the slums of New York City to reveal the squalid living conditions endured by the unfortunates he called "the other half." The closest any noted photographer of the New Northwest came to Hine's portrait of Luther Watson, for instance, a fourteen-year-old Kentucky boy who had lost his right arm in a veneering saw in a box factory, was probably Asahel Curtis of Seattle, who recorded moody views of slate pickers in a Washington coal mine and of women cannery workers.[5]

To be sure, some of the Northwest's turn-of-the-century photographers skillfully framed and preserved important facets of work life: logging scenes were the specialty of the Kinsey brothers, Darius and Clark; hard-rock mining found two of its most faithful chroniclers in T. N. Barnard and Nellie Stockbridge of Wallace, Idaho; crewmen of the tall ships on Puget Sound often posed for the camera of Wilhelm Hester. But these were exceptions. In fact, even when commercial photographers recorded scenes of work life – as distinct from the more general and impersonal scenes of industry – they tended to compose group shots that served a purpose not unlike that of elementary school portraits today. Pioneer photographers made money selling such images to people who wanted them as mementos or keepsakes.[6]

Few photographers captured the diverse aspects of economic life in the New Northwest better than Asahel Curtis. His portraits of such representative types as loggers, coal miners, harvest hands, and cannery operatives were often quite eloquent, yet he never pretended to make a systematic study of work life. Such images, in fact, comprised but a minuscule portion of his more than sixty thousand negatives.[7]

If the New Northwest's professional photographers did not choose to document work life in all its dimensions, the turn-of-the-cen-

tury amateur was ill-equipped to fill the gap. Inexpensive and crude box cameras often yielded fuzzy and poorly exposed snapshots that had little enduring value. Moreover, unlike the dedicated amateur today who can buy highly automated, lightweight, and relatively compact Nikon or Canon cameras identical to those used by news professionals, the serious photographer a century ago usually required a large and cumbersome camera. Even more intimidating were the technical difficulties that related to proper exposure and development of film and to printing the image, work easily done by a custom laboratory today. Because the photographic process was time consuming and expensive, it is not surprising that few if any turn-of-the-century laborers sought to record scenes of their own lives.[8]

Specially composed and printed albums of photographs became popular in the late nineteenth century. Mathew Brady produced a major one of Civil War scenes; Edward Curtis, the better-known brother of Asahel, produced a multivolume series on American Indians. But photographers of the early Pacific Northwest published no books or albums of images about the region's work life – unlike Brady on the Civil War or his regional contemporaries Carleton Watkins and William Henry Jackson on the scenic wonders of the West. A much less pretentious project was an album of scenes from Indian life prepared by Pendleton, Oregon, photographer Major Leander (Lee) Moorhouse. But though Indians were a popular subject, work life in the New Northwest was not. Nothing comparable to Moorhouse's Indian album was ever compiled on work life, not even to emphasize its heroic side.[9]

Among the many hand-tinted postcards depicting life in the New Northwest was one that purported to show a "typical" Indian village, although in reality there never was anything *typical* about the many different housing styles used by the region's Native Americans. Curi-

8. Women workers at the Apex Fish
Company steam cookers in 1913
presented an idealized image of cannery labor on Puget Sound. Courtesy Special Collections Division,
University of Washington Libraries, A. Curtis no.27677.

9. A railroad construction crew
bakes its daily bread near Terry,
Montana, circa 1909. The photographer was Evelyn Cameron, an
exception to the rule that amateurs
did not produce good images of the
wageworkers' frontier. Living with
her husband on a hardscrabble
ranch in eastern Montana, Cameron became a photographer, developing and printing thousands of
glass-plate negatives in a cavelike
darkroom dug out of a hillside. She
ordered her first camera by mail in
1894, and from then through the
1920s she recorded scenes of every-
day life in eastern Montana. Courtesy Montana Historical Society.

10. "The widow-maker" was a photograph staged to illustrate the dangers inherent in logging. There is no indication that the image was ever published. Courtesy Oregon Historical Society, Drake no.8051.

ously, no one ever attempted to sell a postcard image claiming to depict a *typical* view of work life in the region. In the latter category, everything was defined by reference to specific industries, although, in fact, gangs of laborers – members of the Northwest's army of toilers – *were typical* of work life in all of the region's major industries.

Preserved among the commercial images of work life are beautiful, hand-tinted postcards showing loggers or miners or commercial fishermen at work harvesting the region's prodigious natural resources. There is even a card that shows women confectionery workers. Among the few exceptions to the various photographic idealizations of Northwest work life were scenes of industrial violence in Idaho's Coeur d'Alene mining region recorded by T. N. Barnard. Another rarity was a postcard showing dead men – members of the Industrial Workers of the World and victims of Washington's infamous Everett Massacre of 1916 – that union members distributed to raise funds for their legal defense.

During the early years of urban-industrial society, many more residents of the New Northwest lost their lives through work-related accidents than through all of the region's much-publicized Indian wars combined. In every one of the Pacific Northwest's major industries – and especially in logging, sawmilling, mining, and railroading – danger was omnipresent. But images that reminded viewers that workers suffered maiming or death, or that some of them wintered in shabby enclaves like Seattle's Pioneer Square or Portland's Burnside district, simply found little market. Besides, such images were bold admissions of failure in a region "sold" to prospective settlers, investors, and tourists for its natural beauty, abundant resources, and personal opportunities.

Photographs of work life in the New Northwest reveal in retrospect the complex dimen-

11. Two members of the West's migratory army of workers sew sacks of grain shut in the Palouse country, an area that included eastern Washington and northern Idaho. In other seasons they might have found work as deck hands or as itinerant railroaders ("boomers"). Kevin Starr observed of an earlier generation of wheat workers in California's Central Valley that they "were single men, as were most of the miners, and when they returned from the fields they lived, as did the miners, in shacks or bunkhouses devoid of domesticity. Coming into railheads – Willows, Turlock, Modesto, Hanford – or the shipping towns of the Carquinez Straits on the North Bay, they drank, fought, gambled, and whored as had the miners in Marysville and Sacramento a generation earlier." *Inventing the Dream: California through the Progressive Era* (New York: Oxford University Press, 1985), 132. Courtesy Idaho State Historical Society, no.60.52.813.

sions of something that most people in the early 1900s perceived only as a series of distinct industrial activities, each oriented toward production of an important natural resource. Hence it was all too easy for observers to misunderstand or fail to perceive features of work life *common* to all of the region's major industries. The photographic record, moreover, focuses attention on a place that contemporaries probably understood only vaguely, if at all. Yet the existence of this place explains a great deal about why work life in the natural resource–rich states of Oregon, Washington, Idaho, and Montana was never simply a carbon copy of that in the industrialized East, and why all four states experienced a sometimes troubled passage from rural-agrarian to urban-industrial society during the years between the mid-1880s and the early 1930s.

Strange as it now seems, westerners in those years had no commonly accepted name for this place that at various times extended from the farms and ranches of the Great Plains to the orchards and oil fields of Southern California,

and from the tall timber country of the Pacific Northwest to the metal mines of the Rocky Mountains. Its boundaries encompassed sparsely settled farm districts no less than the crowded hiring halls and saloons of the region's largest cities. It existed, in fact, wherever large numbers of workers gathered to harvest the products of the West's forests, fields, and coastal waters, to mine its precious and base metals, to drill for oil, to load its ships, and to construct its cities, transportation lines, and irrigation systems.[10]

For want of a better name I have termed this place the *wageworkers' frontier*.[11] The twin concepts of wagework and frontier may at first glance seem as unlikely a combination as steel mill and covered wagon. Yet the neologism offers one way to emphasize that concentrated in parts of the West was a veritable army of manual laborers who worked for wages – the modern condition of employees in the United States and western Europe – yet who led lives influenced by attitudes and patterns of behavior rooted in the region's recent past. It is the

expansion and contraction of the wageworkers' frontier, moreover, that clearly helps to account for the once peculiar demographic composition of the New Northwest's work force and for some unusual turns and twists in the course of its labor organization.[12]

Although boundaries of the wageworkers' frontier never appeared on any census map and apparently shifted with each passing year, the area's existence can still be confirmed through population statistics, anecdotal accounts, and old photographs. Such evidence, in addition, suggests that this was not only a place but also a state of mind. That is, the West of the wageworkers' frontier was often popularly equated with great personal opportunity, and many a worker who traveled there was no less influenced by romantic notions of success than the stereotypical agrarian pioneer who plodded overland in search of a "promised land."[13]

Some mines and mills of the wageworkers' frontier were actually larger and more heavily

12. Workers in Tacoma's Atlas Foundry. These men were typical of employees in the various manufacturing plants and mills that clustered in cities around the New Northwest, workers who attracted far less public attention than the region's ubiquitous loggers, miners, and harvest hands. In 1909 there were approximately 120,000 wageworkers in manufacturing plants of all types in the New Northwest, and they earned an average annual wage of $731 (the national average was about $500). Metal and coal mining in the four states employed another 32,525 wageworkers. Courtesy Tacoma Public Library, Northwest Room, no.258x.

13. Recalling the classic West: the Montana photographer L. A. Huffman photographed White Bull, a Cheyenne, being interviewed by O. D. Wheeler, June 20, 1901, regarding details of the Custer battle a quarter century earlier. Courtesy Montana Historical Society, Huffman no.981-142.

capitalized than those in the East and Midwest, but when sophisticated technology combined with a physical setting that still seemed wild and inhospitable and a social structure that still seemed flexible, it frequently created the impression among immigrants from the East that in the West anything was possible. Belief in America's Horatio Alger success myth apparently intensified on the wageworkers' frontier, where, according to a popular adage, the man wielding the pick and shovel today might one day, with a little luck and hard work, become the boss. Sometimes that did happen, as in the case of the Butte copper baron Marcus Daly, but far more common was the western wage earner who kept searching for but never quite realizing his dream of success. More than one militant labor organization attracted a follow-

ing by promising to resolve the tension between western myth and reality.[14]

The classic or frontier West has not usually been closely associated with wagework. The classic West, in the words of the historian Richard Maxwell Brown, was the "pioneer West or the old West, with its distinctive mythology focusing on mountain men, cowboys, Indians, prospectors, gunfighters, and outlaws." Presumably, any sizable community of wageworkers belonged to what Brown called the counterclassic West of urbanization, industrialization, and technological advancement. In actuality, however, the two Wests overlapped frequently, and one such intersection was the wageworkers' frontier. When, for instance, the gunslinger mentality of the classic West was employed in the complex new business of labor

relations, the result was often industrial violence.[15]

One particularly colorful embodiment of the overlap between the two Wests was Charles Siringo, the self-described "cowboy detective," who acted out his classic West fantasies in a labor dispute that convulsed Idaho's Coeur d'Alene mining district in 1892. When mineowners hired the Pinkerton agent to spy on union meetings, he succeeded beyond their wildest dreams. Adopting the alias C. Leon Allison, Siringo took a job at the Gem Mine, joined the local miners' union, and seemed to be one of its most earnest members. His fellow workers soon elected him recording secretary, a position that for seven months allowed him access to the union's innermost secrets. These he dutifully passed on to his employers under cover of darkness. When union members were thwarted once too often by mineowners who seemed to anticipate their every move, they became suspicious and finally unmasked Siringo. The detective eluded an angry mob when he slipped through a hole sawed in the floor of his rooming house and crawled under the board sidewalk to a nearby creek and freedom. But his treachery angered miners and triggered violent retaliation against the owners.

Another throwback to the classic West was M. C. Sullivan, head of a private detective agency in Portland, Oregon. For a fee, he and his operatives would infiltrate the region's newly organized labor unions, intimidate employees, and supply their corporate masters with private armies. Sullivan was especially proud of the time in 1891 when he helped lure unsuspecting blacks from the Midwest to coal mines east of Seattle, where under the watchful eyes of his troops they were pressed into service as strikebreakers in defiance of Washington's state constitution, which forbade the creation of private armies.

"Where is your authority, Mr. Sullivan, for bringing an armed body of men into this coun-

Violent Rhetoric of the Classic West

I was listening to yarns in the smoking-compartment of the Pullman all the way to Helena [in 1889], and with very few exceptions, each had for its point, violent, brutal, and ruffianly murder — murder by fraud and the craft of the savage — murder unavenged by the law, or at the most by an outbreak of fresh lawlessness. At the end of each tale I was assured that the old days had passed away, and that these were anecdotes of five years standing. One man in particular distinguished himself by holding up to admiration the exploits of some cowboys of his acquaintance, and their skill in the use of the revolver. Each tale of horror wound up with "and that's the sort of man he was," as who should say: "Go and do likewise."
– Rudyard Kipling, *American Notes* (1890; Boston: Brown and Co., 1899), 78–89

try?" asked a Seattle newspaper reporter.

"Carry it in my vest pocket, sir," was the detective's reply. "It requires a little nerve and a pat hand and the grit to stand by it and [a gun] in your vest pocket." Sullivan's response was perhaps a reflection of the fact that earlier in his career he had driven a stagecoach in Nevada and generally bullied his way through life and swaggered in the manner popularly attributed to Euro-American males of the classic West.[16]

It should be emphasized that certain features of the wageworkers' frontier were similar to those found in other regions of the United States or in the country as a whole. Spies like Siringo and thugs like Sullivan were by no means limited to labor relations in the New Northwest. Likewise, the image of "Golden America" was fixed in the minds of immigrants regardless of whether their destination was East or West. But on the wageworkers' frontier, individual behavior, national beliefs, and

14. L. A. Huffman photographed Montana cowboys at a chuck wagon in the mid-1880s. The land was no longer frontier, but neither was it urban or industrialized. The labor leader William D. Haywood, himself once a cowboy in Nevada, later recalled: "A cowboy's life is not the joyous existence shown in the motion pictures, read about in cheap novels, or to be seen in World's Exhibitions. The cowboy's work begins at daybreak. If he is on the ranch he rolls out of bed, slips on his pants, boots and hat and goes to the barn to feed his saddle horses. It is his greatest pride that he does not work on foot." *Bill Haywood's Book* (New York: International Publishers, 1929), 33. Courtesy Montana Historical Society, no.981-570.

15. Charles A. Siringo, "The Cowboy Detective." He wrote in his autobiography that, after Chicago's Haymarket Riot of 1886, "I commenced to wish that I were a detective so as to help ferret out the thrower of the bomb and his backers. I knew very little about the detective business, though I had spent part of 1881 and 1882 doing secret work for Texas cattlemen against cattle thieves in western Texas and New Mexico. This had given me a taste for the work, and I liked it."

In 1891, after he had become a Pinkerton detective, his supervisor asked him to go to the Coeur d'Alene mining district of northern Idaho, explaining that "the Miners' Union of that district was raising Hades with the mine-owners who had formed themselves into a Mine-Owners Association for self-protection, and that the association wanted a good operative to join the Miners' Union so as to be on the inside of the order when the fast approaching eruption occurred." *A Cowboy Detective* (1912; rpt. Lincoln: University of Nebraska Press, 1989), 12, 135-36. Courtesy Idaho State Historical Society, no.80-125.1

16. After outbursts of industrial violence in 1892 and 1899, mineowners in the Coeur d'Alene district resorted to work permits. A miner could obtain the red work permit card only after swearing an antiunion pledge before Dr. Hugh France, county coroner and supporter of the mineowners. Without the card there was no job. The state-backed permit system continued until January 1901, when Idaho's new governor, Frank Hunt, abolished the practice. Courtesy Idaho State Historical Society, no.63-5736.

17. An island on the land: the young community of Aberdeen on Gray's Harbor in Washington's timber country. The settlement dated from 1884 when a sawmill was erected and the townsite platted. By the early twentieth century, Aberdeen together with its sister city, Hoquiam, formed a major center for logging and sawmilling. "For Grays Harbor, the early years of the century were busy and exciting, despite recurrent depressions of the lumber market. Sawmills and woodworking plants of various kinds were constructed; jerry-built homes were hastily erected to accommodate the flood of loggers. The shipyards were active too." *Washington, A Guide to the Evergreen State* (Portland: Binfords & Mort, 1941), 69. Courtesy Historical Photograph Collections, Washington State University Libraries, Pratsch no.40.

PERMIT TO SEEK EMPLOYMENT.

No. 1303   June 8   1900.

This is to certify that Jno F Hawker,

a laborer by occupation, is qualified under the proclamation issued by order of the Governor of Idaho, May 8th, 1899, to seek employment in any of the mines in Shoshone County and has permission by virtue hereof to do so. This card is to be deposited with the manager or superintendent of the mine where the person above named is employed, and must be held for purpose of periodical inspection pursuant to the terms of the aforesaid proclamation.
Witness my hand this 8 *day of* June   1900.

DR. HUGH FRANCE.

By Geo F Edmiston Deputy.

social patterns had a way of becoming exaggerated or distorted to create statistical or historical anomalies. One of the most obvious of these deviations from the national norm was the unusually large number of young single males who populated the wageworkers' frontier and who maintained an itinerant way of life there.[17]

Some workers inhabited communities that physically resembled factory towns in Pennsylvania or Massachusetts, yet which were still rooted in the settlement pattern typical of the classic West. That is, these communities formed an integral part of a regional pattern in which a few large cities economically dominated urban outposts scattered across a vast and lightly populated hinterland. By rail more than 770 miles separated Portland and San Francisco in the early twentieth century, and between those two cities lay forests, fields, and mountains – but only a few real population centers. An equal distance and an even more sparsely inhabited terrain separated San Fran-

cisco and Salt Lake City as surely as if they were two islands afloat in the vast Pacific.

Various maps that accompany the 1900 federal census clearly delineate the region's peculiar island pattern of settlement. A Euro-American population that appeared to flow steadily west from the Atlantic seaboard to form a more or less continuous area of settlement fractured once it reached the dry country west of the 100th meridian to create dozens of little islands. This pattern of settlement was less distinct in the New Northwest, but even in that generally well-watered land, settled areas still tended to resemble islands separated by miles of dense forests, uninhabited mountain ranges, and sagebrush-covered plains. Many of the islands on the land were visual reminders not only of the peculiar features of western climate and topography but also of a regional economy that as late as World War I was still closely tied to production of natural resources often found in remote, nearly inaccessible places.

Aberdeen.
Grays Harbor

18. Butte, Montana, heart of the copper kingdom that stretched from Alaska to Mexico. As of 1925, Butte alone had produced one-quarter of all copper mined in the United States, a total of 8.9 billion pounds. For several decades it was also the largest city in Montana. Joseph Kinsey Howard once described this island on the land as "sprawling and slovenly, a bully of a city, stridently male, profane and blustering and boastful: 'The biggest mining camp in the world!' 'A mile high and a mile deep!' 'The richest hill on earth!'" *Montana: High, Wide, and Handsome* (1943; rpt. Lincoln: University of Nebraska Press, 1983, 85. Courtesy Minnesota Historical Society, no. 54120.

Hard Places

The road to Silver City [Idaho] was through a country that was rugged, bleak, and gray. No habitations except the occasional stations, most of them deserted, and a farm here and there. Not a tree to be seen in the entire distance, nothing but crooked, gnarled sagebrush, greasewood and stretches of browse. At least this was true until one came to the river; there the country was broken up into foot-hills with high mountains behind them. – William D. Haywood, *Bill Haywood's Book* (New York: International Publishers, 1929), 56

The settlement pattern together with the newness of many communities meant that workers in places like the mining camps of Arizona and Montana or the timber towns of the Pacific Northwest lived in close proximity both in time and place to attitudes and ways of life rooted in the classic American West. As the historian David Emmons noted in his study of the West's single most important mining center: "Butte managed to combine the presumed chaos of the frontier with the confusion of industrialization."[18]

There was no way in the West to replicate the world of workers as it existed in 200-hundred-year-old eastern communities dominated by well-established agricultural and commercial elites who, for instance, might have used their surplus capital to start a local mill complex. For Butte and most other communities on the wageworkers' frontier, there would be no "clumsy and halting transition from preindustrial village to industrial town." In fact, as Emmons observed of the Irish who dominated the mines of early Butte: "Not only did they encounter no hostile and entrenched society upon their arrival, they encountered no society at all."[19]

Undoubtedly the single most distinguishing feature of the wageworkers' frontier was the army of itinerant laborers who were constantly shifting from place to place and from job to job. Before the First World War the harvest of wheat alone required thousands of workers each season, and every hundred miles of railway line required an average of 156 workers to maintain it. The swelling ranks and apparently ceaseless wanderings of these laborers did not go unremarked in the West, but like the wageworkers' frontier itself, itinerancy was a phenomenon that had no commonly accepted name. Some contemporaries who commented on the migrants dismissed them as tramps and hoboes; the economist Carleton Parker, one of the few scholars who studied their lives firsthand, would label them "casual laborers."[20]

Indeed, some were casual about work, and some were hoboes and tramps. But many of those in the ranks of the mobile army of labor were at best unwilling conscripts who were ready and able to take steady jobs, if only such jobs could be found. The itinerants were in many ways no different from the unemployed of Chicago, New York, or Boston, who upon losing a job might trudge down the street in search of another. Their counterparts on the wageworkers' frontier, however, were certainly more visible and perhaps more volatile because the loss of a job in one of the West's natural resource–based communities often meant having to relocate to another island community some distance away to find work.[21]

A slump in the price of copper, for instance, might close mines in Butte and dozens of other outposts in the West's copper kingdom and send hundreds, even thousands, of miners out looking for work in other camps, or sometimes even in other industries. Having little money, the job seekers usually traveled inside, atop, and beneath railway freight cars, and often they congregated in highly visible worker enclaves that could be found in every major city

The Copper Kingdom

The Butte citizen's blood pressure rises and falls with the price of copper. He opposes war "and yet, when you come to think of it, war would probably raise the price of copper and increase work and wages. . . ." Sometimes he is half-convinced that Butte is the real capital of the United States and copper instead of gold the proper standard of values. — *Montana, A State Guide Book* **(New York: Viking Press, 1939), 8**

in the region. It was all too easy for observers to lump many distinct categories of workers under the common banner of casual laborers.[22]

Another distinguishing characteristic of labor in the New Northwest was the way that manual workers divided into three encompassing categories: craftsmen, operatives, and laborers. The same tripartite division occurred in other parts of the United States, but the still developing and thus labor-intensive Northwest had a much higher ratio of laborers to craftsmen, for instance, than was typical of older, more developed parts of the United States, and many fewer women and children in its total work force. Craftsmen were the printers, painters, plumbers, masons, carpenters, and other skilled workers who could be found in urban centers. Operatives were the men and women who ran the machines in sawmills, canneries, and other manufacturing establishments. Although they developed considerable manual dexterity in performing repetitive tasks, most operatives were not highly skilled in the same way that craftsmen were. In some cases the work had once been done by craftsmen, but machine production opened the way for the less skilled but highly proficient operatives. Among the operatives

most noted for their dexterity were the shingle weavers of the New Northwest, who worked with such speed that they appeared to be weaving their product into overlapping bundles.[23]

Many operatives were young adults, for whom tending machines was but a step on the way to some other shill or economic status. Unlike the ranks of laborers and craftsmen, those of operatives included women who did all types of machine work, from running sewing machines in the region's garment factories and staffing telephone switchboards to laboring in fish canneries or stuffing sausages on a production line, to name only a few of the industrial processes that employed women.

In many ways the lives of operatives and craftsmen in the urban Northwest and the urban East were not very different. Yet even the world of the Northwest's operatives and craftsmen was shaped to some degree by the army of laborers who seemed forever on the move across the wageworkers' frontier that often lay at their very doorstep. It is these workers, the itinerant laborers whose presence could be measured throughout the region in terms of competition for jobs, wage rates, and labor organization, who are the primary subject of the following chapter.[24]

Although the wageworkers' frontier lasted into the 1920s in some areas, it seemed forever in transition: no longer classic frontier West but distinct from the industrial East and Midwest. The word *juxtaposition* probably best describes this state of flux: the latest industrial processes and technologies were juxtaposed to a physical setting that in some ways had changed little from the early days of Euro-American exploration; the present was juxtaposed to elements of life and ways of thinking typical of the classic West; and the dependency inherent in wage work was juxtaposed to dreams of personal freedom and success that were part of the Golden West mythology.[25]

19. A typical Northwest lumber camp, this one was located on a remote tributary of Idaho's "shadowy" St. Joe River. The dress of loggers was both distinctive and functional. By the early part of the twentieth century, they invariably wore calked ("cork") boots and stag pants held in place by suspenders. The trousers, made of pure wool so closely woven as to be almost waterproof, were also known as tin pants because incrustations of dirt and sweat enabled them to stand up by themselves, or so at least some observers claimed. Cut off high above the ankles to avoid underbrush, they were also known as high-water pants. "The calk boots, needed for sure footing in the woods, barred him from any decent floor, for the points wore holes in the wood. On the Seattle-Tacoma boats a sign, 'No Calk Boots on the Upper Deck,' confined the logger to the lower depths," recalled Harvey O'Connor in his memoir, *Revolution in Seattle* (1964, rpt. Seattle: Left Bank Books, 1981), 63. Some establishments frequented by loggers provided shingles or pieces of old automobile tires for them to step on and walk or slide along in order to protect the floor. Courtesy Historical Photograph Collections, Washington State University Libraries, no. 70-0099.

20. Garment workers in Spokane were photographed in a setting more commonly associated with the industrial East. Although some women in the New Northwest were manual workers – manufacturing operatives rather than skilled craftsmen or casual laborers – many wage-earning women held jobs as nurses, teachers, and clerks. The federal census for 1900 recorded that female breadwinners in the continental United States composed 14.3 percent of the total work force; women numbered only 11.1 percent of the total in the West but 17.5 percent in states of the Atlantic seaboard. Courtesy Eastern Washington State Historical Society, no.L85-79.133.

21. Juxtaposing modern industrial technology to a classic frontier setting was Wickes, a mining and smelter camp photographed in 1886. Located in the mountains south of Helena, the community boasted the first lead-silver smelter in Montana. Courtesy Haynes Foundation Collection, Montana Historical Society, Haynes no.1747.

22. Washington coal miners on the morning shift. Coal mines were concentrated on both sides of the Cascades – east of Tacoma, Seattle, and Bellingham, and west of Ellensburg – and Washington was the leading coal producer in the New Northwest. Coal was also mined commercially in Montana and for a brief time on the Oregon coast near Coos Bay. Output from Washington's coal mines peaked in 1918 at 4.1 million short tons and declined after that as the state's major market, San Francisco, switched to increasingly plentiful California oil. In 1909 the coal mines of Oregon, Washington, and Montana employed approximately eleven thousand men. Courtesy Special Collections Division, University of Washington Libraries, A. Curtis no.14713.

Scenes of Work Life That No Photograph Showed: I

January 2 – J. M. Macghee, age 37, married; fatally injured by being caught in a revolving shaft that conveys power from a Pelton wheel to the machinery. He was in the act of oiling the bearings of the shaft when his clothing became fast to it. He was carried around with each revolution until he was completely stripped of his clothing, and his unconscious body was thrown to the ground below. He died in half an hour after receiving the injuries. The coroner decided that it was purely accidental, and no inquest was held.

February 4 – David Evans, age 30, married; killed by a trip [string] of cars in the New Castle slope. He was employed as a roller man, whose duty was to keep the rollers, etc., in repair. He was engaged in fixing some of these when an empty trip that was descending the slope ran over him, mutilating his body terribly. It seems that the deceased was very reckless, as he was in the habit of jumping on the cars as they passed him in the slope, going at a high rate of speed. He had been warned by his fellow-workmen from doing so and from going on the track while they were hoisting, but he still persisted in doing so, thus causing his untimely death.

March 15 – Peter Gara, age 50, married; fatally injured by riding up No.12 slope of the Black Diamond mines. He and others were riding on an empty trip of cars, going to their dinner. The front car got off the track and was pulled against the timber. The hook on the chain became straightened and the trip ran down the slope a short distance; he jumped out of the car, and in so doing he fell under the cars, injuring his spinal column. He died two days after being injured. – List of fatalities, Washington State, *Annual Reports of Coal Mine Inspectors,* 1893 (Olympia, 1894), 39–40

23. The kind of image that never appeared in the promotional literature: removing bodies following the Wellington disaster of March 1, 1910, when an avalanche struck two Great Northern trains parked near the west portal of Cascade Tunnel. Snow swept them down the mountain slope into the Tye Valley and killed ninety-six passengers. Only eight passengers and fourteen crewmen and postal employees survived the New Northwest's worst railway accident. Courtesy Special Collections Division, University of Washington Libraries, A. Curtis no. 17465.

Scenes of Work Life That No Photograph Showed: II

Coal mine explosions claimed 45 lives in Roslyn, Washington, in May 1892 and another 31 in Carbonado in 1899. In August 1894 a fire at Franklin killed 37 miners:

The first news of the mine disaster reached Seattle about 1 o'clock. At 2:20 a special train conveying Superintendent Smith and Mine Superintendent T. B. Corey left, arriving at Franklin about 4 P.M. The regular 4:30 passenger for Franklin was delayed nearly an hour at Seattle. Aboard it were Andrew F. Burleigh, general counsel; Prosecuting Attorney John F. Miller, Coroner George M. Horton, Undertakers James A. Greene and E. R. Butter-

worth, Telegraph representatives and the usual number of passengers. The trip was anything but a pleasant one, and some affecting scenes were enacted. It was much like a funeral train. Mr. Burleigh likened it to a house of mourning. Women were screaming, strong men shed tears of sorrow and babies cried piteously. Many of the passengers had near and dear relatives at work in the mine. With some it was a brother of theirs, a son or perchance a sweetheart. Mr. and Mrs. Hall, an elderly couple, got on the train in Renton. The wife and mother was sobbing bitterly. They had a son, one of the 37 victims of the mine horror. – Seattle *Telegraph,* Aug. 25, 1894, p. 1

Dimensions of the Wageworkers' Frontier

CHAPTER 2

The "frontier" has now disappeared and the loss of it is a calamity. It meant cheap or free land to the landless, adventure for the restless, a new chance in life for the beaten, a school for the development of a free, unconventional American manhood and womanhood. – Former President Benjamin Harrison to students of Stanford University, March 1894

I learned a great deal about the lives of the migratory workers. The majority were American-born Eastern youth of adventurist spirit, who had followed Horace Greeley's advice: "Go West, young man and grow up with the country!" Out there they became floaters, without homes or families. – Elizabeth Gurley Flynn, *The Rebel Girl* (1973)

The physical dimensions of the wageworkers' frontier of the Pacific Northwest fluctuated over time, especially as the region became more urbanized. This frontier expanded as new agricultural lands and timber and mining camps opened, and it contracted with depletion of natural resources or when one of the raw, socially unstable communities matured and became permanent. Numerous ghost towns are vivid reminders that community survival was by no means guaranteed.

The wageworkers' frontier actually originated with the California gold rush of 1848–49, when thousands of restless young men headed west to the diggings. With little capital required to purchase necessary equipment and supplies, early miners were essentially footloose, independent entrepreneurs working small placer claims. But the situation changed when more expensive forms of placer mining and then lode or hard-rock mining were introduced. Flumes, tunnels, stamp mills, and smelters were beyond the means of most individuals and even many partnerships. Lonely, unkempt prospectors remained central figures in western folklore, but more typical were individuals who came west seeking their fortunes as prospectors and ended up employees in one

of the region's new, heavily capitalized mining companies.[1]

Beginning in the 1850s many itinerant laborers drifted in and out of San Francisco, which, despite its cosmopolitan character, was for several decades an integral part of the wageworkers' frontier and home during off-seasons and hard times to an army of jobless men. Hordes of itinerant unemployed laborers choked the local job market, intensified competition for work, and depressed wages. Conversely, during boom times, high wages in the mines drove up the pay scale in San Francisco as well as in the agricultural areas that bordered mining regions. This would become a familiar pattern throughout the West.[2]

The physical boundaries of the wageworkers' frontier probably extended farthest during the opening decade of the twentieth century when the timber frontier moved west from the Great Lakes to the New Northwest and the last major segments of the region's railroad network were spiked into place. In fact, except for early-day manifestations in the hard-rock mining country and in the timber and coal towns of the North Pacific coast and Puget Sound that depended on sail and steamships to reach the outside world, the wageworkers'

24. Railroad tracks formed an industrial corridor through towns like Hope, Idaho, which in 1891 was a division point on the Northern Pacific Railroad. By 1900 few settlements of consequence existed in the New Northwest away from the twin ribbons of steel. At their peak, the railway lines formed a 17,000-mile-long network across the four-state region. Courtesy Montana Historical Society, Haynes no. 2632.

25. A stack of bedrolls or bindles. Many of the New Northwest's itinerant workers hiked from job to job carrying all their personal possessions in their bindles. When the bindle stiff or blanket stiff arrived at an isolated logging camp, he worked a ten-hour day and, as of 1910, earned between seventeen and twenty cents an hour. From his pay, a dollar a month was sometimes deducted for the rudimentary medical care available in some camps. In the bunkhouse he slept in a vermin-infested bed that was often little more than a wooden box filled with straw (a mattress was sometimes available for fifty cents a month). In some camps workers slept two to a bunk. Courtesy Idaho State Historical Society, no. 60-52.93.

frontier was a product of the steel rail. A map in 1900 would have shown railroad lines – "metropolitan corridors" – crossing open spaces to link together a series of dots representing mining and lumber camps, smelter and sawmill towns, and concentrations of ranches and orchards. Less easily depicted would be the temporary communities of men who harvested grain, fruit, and vegetables or graded new railway lines, built dams, and dug irrigation canals, and then dispersed to gather on other jobs or to lay over for the winter in one of itinerant labor's urban enclaves. On the map some dots clustered together would represent the mining camps of Arizona, Colorado, or Montana; the orchards of Washington's Yakima Valley, and the factories in the fields of California's Central Valley. The dots bore names like Bisbee and Jerome, Arizona; Cripple Creek and Leadville, Colorado; Butte and Anaconda, Montana; and Aberdeen and Hoquiam, Washington.[3]

Laborers on the wageworkers' frontier usually worked in all-male gangs and supplied strong arms and backs. They functioned as "human machines" who exchanged physical labor for a daily wage. Their work was invariably heavy, dirty, and often dangerous; their hours were interminably long, often lasting from daybreak until sunset. Loggers typically worked six days a week, ten hours a day. Employers of manual labor ranged from individual farmers and ranchers to heavily capitalized logging and mining operations, although one of the most important sources of work was the West's ubiquitous construction industry.

Some laborers remained in a single industry and gained considerable proficiency as miners or loggers, and in some cases they even bought houses and got married, but in most instances

Blanket Stiffs

When I was a boy I was walking one day in Portland, Oregon, with my father when some day-laborers came swinging into town with their blankets on their backs.

"Look at those tramps," I said with boyish snobbery.

"What tramps?" my father asked.

"Those tramps carrying the blankets."

"Those are not tramps," my father responded. "They are men looking for work. You must not speak contemptuously of men just because they are roughly dressed and out of a job."

As they passed my father gave each of them a cheery greeting. Then, with a fine simplicity, and with the object, I fancy, of giving me a proper lesson in democracy, he said,

"My son, I also have carried my blankets on my back." – Arno Dosch, "Self-Help for the Hobo," *Sunset* 36 (January 1916), 10

the work was not steady. The average job duration among laborers of the West Coast in 1914 was fifteen to thirty days in lumber camps, sixty days in mining, ten days in construction work, and seven days in harvesting. In extreme cases, an itinerant laborer might remain on the job for as few as three hours before walking off.[4]

These human machines might further be classified as drillers, blasters, muckers, stationary engineers, pick boys, and others employed in mining; fallers, buckers, choker setters, whistle punks, and others who harvested and processed wood; and the separator men, oilers, team drivers, sack sewers, and other members of a harvest crew. Joining them was a mixed lot of itinerant railroaders, construction workers, longshoremen, seamen, and general casual laborers.

Little is known about most of these men, although at least one of them, William O. Douglas, eventually became a justice of the United States Supreme Court. On the eve of World War I, young Douglas harvested wheat in eastern Washington. He recalled a fellow laborer named Blacky, a man perhaps thirty years old, who kept all his worldly possessions – a pair of high-heeled shoes bought for a girlfriend in Seattle and a single shirt – in an old, battered suitcase. To Douglas, Blacky was typical of those itinerants likely to remain permanently anchored in this class of manual labor. Others, possessing a bit more skill and drive, circulated freely from one job category to another, for occupational boundaries in all but the most skilled trades did not mean much on the wageworkers' frontier. Because of the high rate of hirings and firings, a common saying in both timber and railroad construction camps was that there were three crews connected with any job: "one coming, one going, one on the job."[5]

There were several reasons for the New Northwest's rapid labor turnover. Some itinerants were social misfits, some were chronic alcoholics, some were restless by nature, and some changed jobs because of harsh and arbitrary employers. All were kept on the move by a frequent surplus of labor in one locality or by reports of high wages being paid somewhere else. Probably contributing to rootlessness was their initial move west, which in itself meant the temporary loss of close and stabilizing ties of family, neighborhood, and church. Workers could not establish roots when their jobs were short term or where the community was no more than an isolated work site lacking all but the most rudimentary social and cultural life.

Perhaps the single most important reason for widespread itinerancy among western laborers was the cyclical nature of the region's essentially colonial economy. The New Northwest was forever at the mercy of market prices paid for its basic commodities. The population of the Rocky Mountain and Pacific states, which constituted a mere 5 percent of the national total in 1900, was simply too small to absorb the region's outpouring of raw materials. In every major industry, important markets and sources of investment capital were both located outside the region. This colonial relationship together with the boom-and-bust economy heightened workers' sense of dependency and encouraged their mobility.

Besides the cycles of a natural resource–based economy, another basic rhythm kept laborers on the move: seasonal alternations between work and unemployment. With the melting of winter snows in March or April, the timber industry sprang to life, reached a peak of activity in late summer, then tapered off in late October or early November. In many places the mining industry, too, worked from spring until fall but slumbered when weather conditions isolated and idled the mines. The wheat harvest in August and September created a brief but insatiable demand for labor. With the change of seasons, laborers flowed in

Lumber as a Cyclical Business

Mr. Page. **A great many of the mills are idle. To illustrate the lumber business, we have been in the lumber business for 19 years. Out of the 19 years we have been closed down 9 on account of the price of lumber.**

Acting Chairman Commons. **Closed down 9?**

Mr. Page. **We have been running 19 years, closed down 9, and running 10.**

– Testimony of Paul E. Page, president of Page Lumber Company, Seattle, Washington, August 1914, *Report of the Commission on Industrial Relations* 64th Cong., 1st Sess., 1916, Senate Document 415, vol. 5, p. 4266

26. A typical harvest crew in the early twentieth century. Vestiges of this way of life could still be observed in the late 1930s: "West of Pendleton is a section of the vast wheat region of the Inland Empire. In this area two million acres of wheatlands are under cultivation, and one might walk from Pendleton to The Dalles through growing grain. Early spring, tractors, drag plows, harrows, and drills cross rich brown fields; late summer and early fall, combines drawn by tractors, mules, or horses, harvest the grain. Occasionally 32 horses are handled with one pair of reins as a combine travels around the golden foothills, cutting, threshing, and sacking, exemplifying modern efficiency at its peak, in marked contrast with a scythe and cradle used by pioneers. These large-scale operations directed by bronzed harvest crews, are as picturesque as the cattle drives of old." *Oregon: End of the Trail* (Portland: Binfords & Mort, 1940), 261. Courtesy Oregon Historical Society, no.79636.

27. Dalkena Lumber Company, Pend Oreille County, Washington, in 1923. Sawmills with their "wigwam burners" were a common sight in timbered portions of the New Northwest. "The mills employ men who are largely family men. Those men get the preference, and from year to year we have a large number of men that we can always depend on. The contrary rule is in effect in the woods. Those men are very largely drifting men," or so H. G. Miller, a Kalispell, Montana, lumberman, testified before the United States Commission on Industrial Relations in Butte in the summer of 1914. *Report of the Commission on Industrial Relations*, 64th Cong., 1st Sess., 1916, Senate Document 415, vol.4, p.3814. Courtesy Eastern Washington State Historical Society, no.L87-1.24076-23.

28. Dinnertime in camp near Silvana, Washington, in 1905. Loggers customarily ate their meals in silence. The foreman, or "bull of the woods," ruled the camp everywhere but in the cookhouse, where the cook was all-powerful. Courtesy Special Collections Division, University of Washington Libraries, UW no.3114.

29. A steam donkey, or stationary yarding machine, at the Goodyear Logging Company, Clallam County, Washington, in 1919. The large gasoline-powered saw, a forerunner of the modern chainsaw, was used to cut wood to fire the steam boiler that powered the winch. Courtesy Library of Congress, no.11604 2-62 71717.

and out of Spokane, Seattle, Portland, and other urban enclaves like a human tide.

Seasonal and cyclical rhythms of western work life placed a premium on physical mobility and broadened definitions of personal job qualifications as workers moved from one industry and location to another. Many laborers would have preferred to remain solely loggers or miners, but the vast majority simply could not afford to be too closely tied to a particular industry or skill. And so they shifted back and forth from the woods or the docks to mining, construction, or harvesting jobs. As early as 1884 a visitor to the New Northwest observed that "the people of the Pacific coast are strangely nomadic – a fact especially true of the unmarried. You can hardly enter into conversation with a working-man who can not give you some account of almost any settled district west of the Rocky Mountains, often including the Sandwich Islands, Australia, and the Chinese ports."[6]

Closer to home, numerous harvest hands in the eastern portions of Oregon and Washington at the turn of the century were temporary recruits from the ranks of metal miners and longshoremen. Depending on the season a dock worker from Seattle might be found in eastern Washington supplying muscle to sack wheat, and when done he would likely return to the waterfront to help load the grain aboard ships. During the course of the year a "tramp" metal miner might move from Bisbee, Arizona, to the Coeur d'Alene district in Idaho, and even on to mines in Alaska. Similar cycles were observed among laborers on a construction gang, who worked in Ohio in the spring, in wheat fields of the Dakotas in fall, in the orange groves of California in winter, and the following summer as stevedores on the Great Lakes.[7]

In Puget Sound's timber country, it was common for laborers to shift from work on steam schooners to longshoring, to jobs in the

Cycles of Migration

There is a peculiar type of wandering logger, less often a wandering sawmill worker, who remains with the industry, but has no home or other definite social ties except the very precarious tie which draws him to the city at frequent intervals. After such a trip to town, which nearly always occurs on the Fourth of July and on Christmas, and probably at several other times during the year, the logger seldom returns to the camp from which he went to town. The range of his wanderings may be wide or narrow. Some of these men find the whole Pacific Northwest too small a field for the exercise of their wanderlust; others are content to go from job to job within a very small area. In general, the migratory logger does not circulate between the long-log and the short-log countries [areas east and west of the Cascade mountains], although he may drift all over either region. For most of them, however, a small field is usually the limit of their wanderings. A logger may have worked in every important camp on Puget Sound and Grays Harbor, but he will seldom leave that region. – Cloice R. Howd, "Industrial Relations in the West Coast Lumber Industry," *Bulletin of the United States Bureau of Labor Statistics no. 349* (1923), 52–53

woods, and then back again to the docks. In the early 1930s one observer noted that in Portland, Oregon, former loggers who had formerly maintained ties to the radical Industrial Workers of the World were "one of the chief sources of the left wing ideology that so permeates the [longshoremen's] union."[8]

Laborers typically traveled overland from job to job by stealing aboard empty boxcars, known as "side-door Pullmans," or by riding the trucks and bolstering rods underneath the

Riding the Trucks

Riding the trucks [wheel assembly] was something that only experienced hoboes ventured. It was packed full of danger. One had to know precisely what he was about, or face disaster. Even with all his skill he might easily be cut to pieces. When a 'bo climbed into the trucks he usually had only a minute or two to do so, and if, once inside, he found he had made a mistake and there was no place for him to ride in that particular kind of truck, he was a good candidate for Potter's Field, and he would hardly have time to get out before the train started.

My first ride on the trucks was on the Northern Pacific, between Missoula and Butte, Montana, on my way to New York. I'll never forget the experience. I had made two coast-to-coast trips already and considered myself an expert hobo, before I finally ventured upon trying the trucks, my favorite riding place on rattlers [fast freight trains] being the tops.

Missoula was a tough town at the time, with hostile shacks [brakemen] and bulls [railroad police], and there was no chance to ride a freight or the tops of a rattler. So I decided to hit the trucks. It was about a three-hour ride to Butte. But just how to get into the trucks was not altogether clear. I had no time to lose, as the passenger train was about to pull out. Selecting a rear car, I crawled over the brakebeam and across the axle. I was now in the very heart of the truck. I had to figure out instantly how to place myself in order to ride, for the train began to move. To get out alive from the truck would now have been impossible. . . .

As the train rapidly gained headway, the one-inch brakerod I was sitting on sagged heavily under my weight. The car rumbled over a switch, and the rod cleared the rails by hardly more than an inch or two. My heart "popped into my mouth." I shivered at such a narrow margin and tried not to think of what would happen to me if the brakerod should come loose, bend down more or break outright, or if we should run across one of those pieces of wire that are frequently to be found snagged in the ballast between the tracks. In any of these cases I should be instantaneously cut to pieces, as hundreds of hoboes had been before me. — William Z. Foster, *Pages from a Worker's Life* (New York: International Publishers, 1939), 118–19

cars. Suspended some ten inches above sudden death, the migrant on a fast-moving train might be blasted with cinders or sand and dust from the West's numerous miles of deserts. To fall asleep meant certain death beneath the wheels. In the winter a worker could sometimes nearly freeze to death riding in open gondolas, and he might be tossed from a moving train by an unsympathetic brakeman or crushed by a shifting load of timber. Fatal accidents reportedly claimed the lives of nearly twenty-five thousand trespassers on railroad property from 1901 to 1905 alone.[9]

Native-born whites among the laborers were often called "hobo" or "tramp" workers because of their migratory life-style. From the employers' perspective, payday was the undoing of such workers. An officer of the Chicago, Burlington & Quincy Railroad complained that too often "the hard earned monthly wage, minus the board and van [room] account, is spent in one glorious week-end spree, while the foreman waits or struggles on with a few weaklings or new men, but without the old hands whom he has worked so carefully or organized into a quickly responding human machine."[10]

Itinerant laborers in the New Northwest

30. Wilhelm Hester photographed Port Blakely, Washington, in the winter of 1905. After Henry Yesler completed the first steam-powered sawmill on Puget Sound in 1853, other mills appeared on various arms of the great waterway. The New Northwest's timber industry initially centered on Puget Sound and the lower Columbia River where "cargo mills" produced the lumber that sailing ships hauled to distant markets. Completion of the Northern Pacific line in 1883 offered access to markets east of the Rocky Mountains, but not until after the turn of the century were railroad rates low enough to allow Pacific Northwest lumber to compete successfully with lumber from the Great Lakes and the South. Even then, most lumber still left the North Pacific coast by ship. Courtesy San Francisco Maritime National Historical Park, Hester no.F20.17,887n1.

31. Workers unloading salmon caught in Washington's Puget Sound. Cannery operations on Puget Sound dated from 1877 and peaked in 1913 with production of 2.5 million cases. A rigid division of labor by race prevailed in the industry: fishermen were predominantly Scandinavians and Finns, who often logged or farmed in the off-seasons; cannery workers were generally Chinese. For many years the lower Columbia River was the center of the region's fishing industry; as late as 1881 there were thirty-five canneries on the river and only two on Puget Sound. Courtesy Photographic Archives, Museum of History and Industry, Seattle, no.10593.

came from a variety of racial and ethnic backgrounds. It was common for immigrants of one nationality to gravitate to certain types of work: Scandinavians, for example, often became loggers, Greeks and Italians worked on railroad construction and maintenance or in the coal mines; and Irish miners predominated for a time in the metal mines of Butte. Asians constituted the largest racial minority; Hispanics were a common part of the work force in the Southwest long before they reached the New Northwest. African Americans were not common, yet racial prejudice against them was pervasive.[11]

A young laborer in a Montana railroad construction camp in the early twentieth century recalled that his crew included about a dozen black workers. The white workers would have little to do with them. When cold weather set in, the whites moved on, but the blacks stayed behind. "Perhaps they feared to leave and make that long walk to Forsyth," speculated Nels Anderson, "passing the all-white camps, feeling strange that far north, and knowing the bias in other camps against them." It was race prejudice, too, that caused unemployed white laborers on Puget Sound to seek to drive hundreds of Chinese laborers from Tacoma and Seattle in the mid-1880s.[12]

Women, who were a major presence in the world of operatives, did not typically hold jobs alongside laborers, especially the itinerants. To be sure, women could be found in any mining camp, although not at first in large numbers. A few arrived as wives, others to manage rooming houses and eating places. Women discovered that skills in cooking, sewing, and laundering could earn them good incomes in the camps. An unknown number of women worked as prostitutes, especially in the predominantly male world of the laborers. Because their numbers were few, women enjoyed great prestige in a mining camp. If the place survived to become a town or village, the ratio

Friends and Enemies

Of the eighteen men who had come in that day [in 1910] on the train to get work, about six were of the northern racial types who called themselves "white men" and held themselves above the Bohunks or foreign migratory workers of whom there were twelve — six Bulgarians, who averaged about 5′ 6″; two Montenegrin giants, three Herzogovenians just as huge and even less literate; and one small Greek we probably would not have hired had we not been urged to do so by Steve Dimitrios, another Greek I had detained in Ashton as messenger and interpreter. Steve spoke fair English and could make a stab at many other languages from central and southern Europe or the Balkans. . . . I could only give orders through Steve, the Greek, who took impish delight in bossing his Bulgarian "enemies." Steve, in fact, was careful to station his small countryman, Joe Papas, where he thought Joe would not come to any harm. — Elliott Paul, *Desperate Scenery* (New York: Random House, 1954), 89–90

of males to females tended to even out as miners got married and raised families.[13]

Although laborers were typically mobile, young, and single, most of them hoped to settle down to a steady job, marry, and have a family. But until that day came, and for some it never did, they continued to live with a large number of men like themselves. In the lumber and railroad camps, they slept in bunkhouses; at some mining operations they lived in company-owned boardinghouses; at some harvest operations they slept in the open. Loggers often lived in camps even more isolated and primitive than those of miners. Logging camps flourished in the early twentieth century, most of them located either on riverbanks or deep in

32. Harvest workers – the team drivers, field pitchers, stationary steam engineers and firemen, separator men, threshers, and laborers who cut, threshed, and sacked wheat – photographed near Moro, Oregon. This crew was unusual in that it contained at least one black member. Courtesy Oregon Historical Society, no.6337.

33. George Keith's logging camp, Wishkah River, Washington Territory. In logging camps, which were essentially makeshift work sites in the woods, there were few females. Some loggers, in fact, regarded a woman in camp as bad luck. Courtesy Historical Photograph Collections, Washington State University Libraries, Pratsch no.350.

34. Ed Dolan's Eagle Dance Hall and Casino, Aberdeen, Washington, was typical of saloons on the wageworkers' frontier. Because of the itinerants' primitive living conditions, many of them regarded such saloons as palaces. Of their usual patrons, Anna Louise Strong wrote that "lumberjacks, a rough and ready type of hard-fighting, hard-working, and hard-drinking labor, agitated and struggled with varying success for decent conditions in the woods. They drifted with winter into the cheap lodging houses near Seattle's vice district, and became the natural prey of prostitutes, employment sharks, vote seekers and agitators. They had a hall of their own, occasionally raided, where hoarse-voiced yells for justice alternated with social evenings." *I Change Worlds* (New York: H. Holt, 1935), 52. Courtesy Historical Photograph Collections, Washington State University Libraries, Pratsch no. 81-003.

the woods alongside the tracks of logging railroads built by timber companies. As the forest was cut, the camps moved too.[14]

As bad as working conditions might be, the environment off the job might be even worse. Because of the seasonal nature of their work, itinerant laborers in the West usually spent at least part of each year in crowded urban enclaves, composed of employment agencies, cheap hotels and lodginghouses, soup kitchens, saloons, and brothels. Every large city had one such district where laborers congregated and survived between jobs. Among the most famous were the Burnside district in Portland and Pioneer Square in Seattle. The urban enclaves were places to rest between jobs, to subsist during the slack winter season, to locate temporary employment in a warehouse or on the docks, or perhaps even to make the transition to the ranks of operatives.[15]

These urban enclaves, like the logging and construction camps, were predominantly male societies. As a result of its close connection with the wageworkers' frontier, Seattle in 1900 recorded the highest percentage of male population among American cities of 25,000 or more (64 percent); Butte, Montana, ranked third (60 percent). It was no accident that both cities featured large and notorious red light districts. Butte's red light district in 1905 was reportedly the second largest in the United States (after New Orleans).[16]

In addition to brothels, saloons were popular institutions among laborers, offering a brief escape from the cramped and dirty quarters that too often typified living arrangements on the wageworkers' frontier. One of the largest and most famous saloons was Erickson's at Second and Burnside in Portland. The men who crowded Erickson's were for the most part loggers and harvest hands, railroad men and miners, fishermen and sailors, prospectors and cowboys. "They were largely workers, do-

On the Road Again

The life of the migratory workers was isolated from that of the stationary workers in the cities. They seldom left the skid row areas of the various cities. They were not welcome "uptown." They traveled by freight cars. Their work was hard and laborious. They were strong and hardy, tanned and weather-beaten by summer suns and winter snows. They regarded the city workers as stay-at-home softies — "scissorbills." They referred to a wife as "the ball and chain." – Elizabeth Gurley Flynn, *The Rebel Girl* rev. ed. (New York: International Publishers, 1973), 103

Erickson's

ERICKSON'S, stretching the full north side of the block on W. Burnside Street between NW. 2nd and NW. 3rd Aves., was once the most widely known saloon in the Pacific Northwest. It is occupied by beer parlors, a restaurant called Erickson's, and a number of other small establishments.

All western states have boasted of places with a "mile long bar" that usually measured a modest hundred feet; but it is a fact that the mahogany in Erickson's saloon ran to 674 feet. Here loggers, seafaring men, dirt movers, and hoboes from everywhere met to drink and talk. When the flood of 1894 swept into the place, proprietor Erickson quickly chartered a scow, anchored it at 2nd and Burnside, stocked it, and business continued more or less as usual. – *Oregon, End of the Trail* (Portland: Binfords & Mort, 1940), 216

ing the hard manual labor of the frontiers, on a temporary spree of enjoyment and making the most of it while money and time were theirs."[17]

During their frequent layovers in the urban enclaves, laborers had ample opportunity to swap stories, share experiences, and absorb social criticism proffered by various radical clubs and newspapers that were invariably a feature of such districts. In this way, though perhaps without fully realizing it, they probed the intellectual dimensions of the wageworkers' frontier. Much of their talk centered on labor discontents, and primary among these was the employment relationship they disparaged as "wage slavery." By the late nineteenth century, work for wages was the usual way to earn a living in the New Northwest, but generally that had not been true before the 1880s, when most people sustained themselves by farming or shopkeeping, not by selling their labor for wages. Enclaves of sawmill workers had existed on Puget Sound since the 1850s, but the employer-employee relationship did not become common in the region until the boom of the 1880s created great demand for hired muscle. The rise of wage work mirrored national trends, yet within the region the sometimes strained relationship between workers and employers occasionally reflected a recent frontier heritage.[18]

Conflict often characterized labor and management relationships on the wageworkers' frontier, as it did in the industrializing world in the East and Midwest. But when conflict erupted in one of the Northwest's island settlements, it was often with the added volatility created when frontier ideals of individualism and personal advancement clashed with the dependency inherent in wage work. Workers – no less than farmers, merchants, and others who moved from the East to the West – seemed to have brought with them a special set of dreams and aspirations. One verse of a popular song that captured the feeling went:

To the west, to the west, to the land of the free
Where mighty Missouri rolls down to the sea;
Where a man is a man if he's willing to toil,
and the humblest may gather the fruits of the soil.[19]

Admittedly, determining what wageworkers thought about their move west is not easy. Unlike the Oregon Trail pioneers, they wrote few personal accounts of their experiences. It seems clear, however, that for many workers the West was not simply a fact of geography but a fantasy created by the promoters of the Golden West. The region's many boosters – the ranks of which included railroad companies, immigration bureaus, and real estate agents – were responsible for an avalanche of promotional literature that nurtured the dream of special opportunity awaiting any wageworker who moved west.[20]

Although most such pamphlets were clearly oriented toward agrarians, the same exaggerated claims of opportunity that fired the imaginations of prospective farmers could also work their magic on wageworkers. The author of one Union Pacific brochure issued in 1889 went so far as to claim of Oregon and Washington:

They entreat the laborer to accept a pleasant home where ample reward for industry surely awaits him; where the opportunities for work are so extensive that the wage-earner has never been driven to seek relief or protection in the "strike," nor the capitalist, to preserve or augment his power, ever resorted to the "lock-out." They offer to the unemployed, and scantily paid working man of the East, who traces his steps along the weary ways of want, a home in a locality where comforts and conveniences combine to lighten labor's task, and placate poverty with plenty.

It was an appealing message, no doubt, but one that deviated considerably from the truth. Of course, even if many of the boosters' claims

Make Money On the New Line

Low rates to points in the Dakotas, Montana, Idaho and Washington, on the **Chicago, Milwaukee & Puget Sound Railway.**

Wonderful opportunities today in farming, fruit growing and mercantile lines, along the newest trans-continental railway.

Complete information and descriptive books free.

F. A. MILLER, General Passenger Agent
Chicago

Chicago
Milwaukee & St. Paul
Railway

[46]

35. Advertising farmland in Montana, the official timetable of the Chicago, Milwaukee & St. Paul Railway for October 1910 employed symbolism that no reader could ignore. A color version of the image showed the farmer plowing up bright gold coins from the fertile soil. Courtesy Milwaukee Road Collection, Milwaukee Public Library.

were totally false, workers living in the East or in Europe probably would not know that. Nor did some workers who moved west understand that the region's generally higher wages reflected an increased cost of living.[21]

Pamphleteers were mythmakers, and effective ones, too. As a group of families prepared to leave Pittsburgh for the New Northwest in the early 1880s, one member responded to a reporter's question about whether they could not continue to make a living in Pennsylvania: "Well, yes, sort of a living. But every year it is becoming more difficult, as the different trades and avocations become more and more crowded by foreign immigrants, giving employers an opportunity to reduce wages. We hear the most encouraging reports from Washington Territory, and believe it is just the place for poor men to go."[22]

The publicists' effectiveness as measured by their potential to swamp the West Coast labor markets with newcomers so alarmed the Oregon Knights of Labor that the organization urged the governor to abolish the state's immigration board, which in the mid-1880s distributed thousands of pamphlets promising that "every man who is able and willing to work with his hands can find some employment at fair wages, especially those who are fitted for farm work. Railroads, public works, mines, mills, logging camps, fisheries and farms all require labor." In the early twentieth century the Butte Miners' Union strongly protested all promotional efforts to attract new workers to Montana, "even those promotions whose ostensible purpose was to fill up the state's agricultural regions." But stopping the avalanche of booster literature proved impossible, and over time, their exaggerated claims and roseate images helped define the intellectual boundaries of the wageworkers' frontier.[23]

One idea popular in late nineteenth-century America was that of the "free-land safety valve." That is, the West's abundant land was

supposed to be freely available to any laborer willing to take up farming. He could thereby emancipate himself from wage slavery and also relieve the discontent of America's industrial workers. Whether this was reality or myth, some workers believed it to be true and acted accordingly. The promises of the promotional literature remained compelling into the early twentieth century, especially for wageworkers unable to see for themselves that much of the best land in the New Northwest was already in the hands of others and that much of the remaining so-called free land was unfit for agriculture.[24]

So powerful was the dream that the 1894 protest platforms and manifestos issued by the Rocky Mountain and Pacific Slope contingents of Coxey's Army – giving voice to the demands of thousands of jobless westerners – called for Congress to provide federal money to irrigate arid land. This, they believed, would provide them work constructing canals and dams as well as an opportunity to claim a well-watered homestead afterwards. In fact, some wageworkers did acquire logged-off and other marginal lands where they lived a hardscrabble existence, alternating between subsistence farming and seasonal jobs in nearby sawmills or railway construction camps.[25]

Giving scholarly sanction to the popular notion of a free-land safety valve was the eminent historian of the American frontier, Frederick Jackson Turner. He asserted in 1903, in one of his most memorable and often quoted essays that "whenever social conditions tended to crystallize in the East, whenever capital tended to press upon labor or political restraints to impede the freedom of the mass there was this gate of escape to the free conditions of the frontier. These free lands promoted individualism, economic equality, freedom to rise, democracy." Turner believed that the era of free land had ended by 1890, and he, like other Americans who shared this conviction, pon-

36. Inventing the dream: "Come Out and Live in Paradise," read an advertisement from the Spokane & Inland Empire Railroad public timetable for February 1911. Courtesy Eastern Washington State Historical Society, no.L88-410.37.

37. Dorothea Lange photographed the dismal landscape associated with stump farming on logged-off land in Idaho's Priest River valley in October 1939. The popular belief was that land fertile enough to grow tall trees would grow good crops, but that simply was not the case.

One early example of the popular belief in land as social security was the admonition that the federal district judge Cornelius H. Hanford of Seattle gave a group of unemployed workers captured in 1894 following their attempt to steal a train to take them to present their "petition in boots" to Congress demanding jobs: "The people who came to this northwest country when my father did, found here no railroads, nor steamboats, nor manufacturing industries to give employment and afford wages . . . and when they met with hard times, instead of going back east making demands on the government for relief, they planted potatoes and peas and cabbage, and preserved themselves and their families from starvation. They set out fruit trees which bore fruit a good deal quicker than any extraordinary measures by which it is [now] proposed to obtain relief." Farmers Loan and Trust Co. et al. vs. Northern Pacific Railway Co. et al. (August Brower et al.) National Archives – Federal Pacific Northwest Region, Seattle. Courtesy Library of Congress, no.LC-USF34-21854-D.

Come Out and Live in Paradise

You can live on your tract in Paradise Valley and retain your position in the city

In case of sickness or accidental injury, we allow purchasers of tracts in Paradise Valley plenty of time to make payments.

Our FREE DEED clause gives to the family of any one who buys a tract in Paradise Valley the best protection obtainable, a free home.

Start that orchard of yours this spring. You do not have to wait until you get a large amount of money saved up, for we are selling Paradise Valley tracts on reasonable terms.

PARADISE VALLEY is on the 5-mile circle, and is composed of exceedingly rich loam soil, sub-irrigated. It lies beautifully, and is thoroughly protected from early and late frosts and high winds.

Paradise Valley Acre Tracts Offer You the Most Ideal Suburban Home

Price of land $400 per acre and up. If desired we will plant to orchard and care for same 4 years. Those who wish to build can take advantage of buying their lumber at a minimum cost from our mill in PARADISE, or if preferred we will contract to build your home on easy terms.

TAKE VERA CAR—GET OFF O.-W. R. & N. CROSSING—15 MINUTE WALK SOUTH.

This coupon is worth money to you.

This represents a cash value of $10.00 on purchase of Paradise Valley Land one coupon for one purchase.

SAVE THIS.

Buy a Home in Paradise

where the Pleasures, Advantages and Conveniences of City and Country Life Combine

For full information fill out and mail this coupon.

Paradise Valley Land Co., Lindelle Bldg., Spokane.

Please send full information to

Name..................

Address..................

Paradise Valley Fruit Land Co.

314-315 Lindelle Bldg., Spokane

38. Laborers on Post Street in downtown Spokane, about 1905. Although Spokane was not a true mining town, like Butte, it was an important service and banking center for metalliferous mining in southern British Columbia and the Inland Empire that was eastern Washington, northern Idaho, and western Montana. It was also a major distribution center for the area's numerous wheat ranches and timber towns. Migratory workers found Spokane full of "employment leeches" or "job sharks." These were the bogus or marginally legitimate employment agencies that flourished by fleecing the casual laborer who sought work in one of the region's extractive industries. A worker occasionally paid for a job that turned out to be nonexistent once he arrived at the work site. Courtesy Eastern Washington State Historical Society, no. L86-1154.

dered the consequences for the United States.[26]

Although in his various writings Turner was relatively circumspect in his evocation of the free-land safety valve concept, some of his disciples were not. They made such exaggerated claims for the efficacy of its operation that they prompted a vigorous counterattack. In one of the most witty of the anti–safety valve critiques, the historian Fred Shannon, in 1945, sought to bury the concept under a mass of statistical evidence suggesting that a far larger number of Americans moved from farm to city than the other way around. Unlike Turner, Shannon saw clearly that wageworkers migrating from the East to the West often remained in a state of dependency, having simply "exchanged drudgery in an Eastern factory for equally ill-paid drudgery (considering living costs) in a Western factory or mine."[27]

What Shannon failed to figure into his equation was the key intellectual component of the wageworkers' frontier: the dreams and aspirations that workers brought west with them. The fact is that some workers traveled west carried along as much by illusion as by railway car or sailing ship. Or, as a Seattle newspaper observed, the newcomers to the New Northwest often believed the region was an Eldorado "where bonanzas lie around loose, and they will pick up a speedy fortune, or at least live easily off the surplus fat of the land."[28]

Many a laborer who moved west would be forced to reconcile the success mythology with the reality of dependency. "Like the pioneers of an earlier day, workingmen who travel westward are for the most part imbued with the restless spirit of enterprise, born of the desire for improved conditions. But unlike the pioneer seeking a homestead and finding it, the modern wage worker who 'goes West' finds no alternative except to hunt for a master," lamented a member of the radical labor union,

Land of Milk and Honey?

Commissioner Garretson. Have you ever in the course of your connection with these questions found anything that led you to believe that a considerable portion of the unemployment, or of the excess of men over positions at a great many portions of the year, were caused by — well, rose-colored advertising of the golden opportunities of the Northwest?
Mr. Swett. Yes. Yes. I positively think so. I believe very, very many people were drawn in this country upon the theory that it was a land of honey and —
Commissioner Garretson. And milk.
Mr. Swett. Milk and Honey.
Commissioner Garretson. Flowing with milk and honey.
Mr. Swett. And they, I say, came in because of the theory that an opportunity for earning a living would be given to every one that would come here, either the opportunity to earn a living or the opportunity to earn a living without striving for it in the extreme degree that is necessary elsewhere.
Commissioner Garretson. They learned when they got here that they had to do their own milking and there was no honey?
Mr. Swett. Yes.
— Testimony of Isaac Swett, executive secretary of the Oregon Civic League, Portland, Oregon, August 1914, *Report of the Commission on Industrial Relations*, 64th Cong., 1st Sess., Senate Document 415, vol.5, pp.4604–5

WASHINGTON

Chicago, Milwaukee & St. Paul Railway.

39. A promotional image by Asahel Curtis, a commercial photographer in Seattle, appeared on the cover of a brochure issued by the Chicago, Milwaukee & St. Paul Railway. This was one of several million brochures issued in the late nineteenth and early twentieth centuries to sell the Great Northwest. A single campaign for the Harriman railroads in the region – the Union Pacific and Southern Pacific – distributed twelve million copies of seventy-five different brochures.

Measuring the impact of promotional brochures is difficult, but imagine for a moment this scene in the home of a discontented iron worker in Pittsburgh in the 1880s. He readjusts the coal-oil lamp to make its light brighter and then reads aloud to his wife and assembled children from one of the pamphlets on the table. From *the Settlers' Guide to Homes in the Northwest – Being a Hand-book of Spokane Falls, Washington Territory* (1885), he reads these words: "To the mechanic we present that grandest opportunity which can ever come to those of this class – the opportunity to secure plenty of labor at good wages." He switches to *The Resources and Attractions of Washington* (1889), an illustrated booklet prepared and distributed by the Union Pacific Railroad, and continues, "Nearly all of the people who have gone to the Pacific Northwest went for the purpose of bettering their condition. Many of them had strong arms and good appetites, but no money in their purse; they had also determination to win and have won." Emma Adams, a visitor to the New Northwest in the late 1880s, observed, "One is simply amazed at the vast amount of money, energy, patience, and persistency there is expended in setting forth the resources, advantages, capabilities, and wonders of this part of the continent." *To and Fro, Up and Down in Southern California, Oregon and Washington, with Sketches in Arizona, New Mexico and British Columbia* (Cincinnati: Cranston & Stowe, 1888), 375. Courtesy Special Collections Division, University of Washington Libraries, UW no.436.

the Industrial Workers of the World, in 1909. Thwarted dreams had a way of creating bitterness, and a worker's belief in the West as a land of unusual opportunity might give rise to a feeling of exploitation when things failed to work out as expected.[29]

In the same way, paradoxically, the popular notion of the Golden West as synonymous with success also imbued some workers with a sense of western advantage, a belief that they were better off than their counterparts in the industrial East. The perception of western advantage occasionally became an effective tool in the hands of labor advocates, who urged the region's workers to organize themselves in order to prevent their being reduced to the downtrodden status of eastern laborers. The fact that wages were often higher in the West only added emphasis to this argument, especially if a believer ignored the increased cost of living that accompanied the higher pay. When Edward Boyce, head of the militant Western Federation of Miners, asserted to the national labor leader Samuel Gompers in the late 1890s that western workers were a hundred years ahead of their eastern comrades, he expressed the sense of western advantage.[30]

Together the intellectual and physical dimensions of the wageworkers' frontier help to explain why labor organization in parts of the New Northwest evolved in ways at odds with developments in the nation's main industrial centers. The clash between harsh reality and unrealistic notions of a Golden West synonymous with success occasionally fostered unrest among the region's workers and gave rise to radical crusades and militant unions like the IWW. The disparity motivated labor's idealists to promote a true commonwealth of toil, "one big union," that through its collective power might at last help disillusioned and discontented workers to realize their elusive dreams of success.

Forging the Commonwealth of Toil

CHAPTER **3**

It is we who plowed the prairies;
   built the cities where they trade;
Dug the mines and built the workshops;
   endless miles of railroad laid.
Now we stand outcast and starving,
   'midst the wonders we have made;
But the Union makes us strong.
– Ralph Chaplin, "Solidarity Forever" (1915)

But we have a glowing dream
Of how fair the world will seem
When each man can live his life secure and
   free;
When the earth is owned by Labor
And there's joy and peace for all
In the Commonwealth of Toil that is to be.
– Ralph Chaplin, "Commonwealth of Toil"
(1918)

Membership in a labor organization was an important facet of work life in the New Northwest, although only a minority of workers ever joined unions. It was the activities of labor unions – their organizing campaigns, their strikes, and their sometimes violent confrontations with recalcitrant management – that more than anything else focused public attention on the world of workers. Violence was sometimes the only thing that forced contemporary society to consider labor's ills, and for that reason it often spurred political protest movements and legislative attempts to redress worker grievances. Even early labor history was written primarily in terms of dramatic episodes.

In retrospect, one labor organization cap-

tured the most attention and lingered longest in the public consciousness of northwesterners. That was the Industrial Workers of the World; its members, Wobblies, demonstrated an uncompromising hostility to capitalism and unorthodox organizing tactics that both frightened and fascinated many onlookers. Even today, many people who know nothing else about the Northwest's labor history know something of the Wobblies, probably because of the violence popularly attributed to them. The western novelist Zane Grey portrayed the Wobblies as pro-German saboteurs of eastern Washington's wheat harvest during the First World War. In *The Desert of Wheat* (1919), Grey's vigilantes lynched a Wobbly organizer and affixed to him a placard bearing the cryptic message, "Last Warning, 3-7-77," the numbers supposed to represent the dimensions of a grave. This was a pointed reference to the Virginia City, Montana, vigilante movement fifty years earlier and to the Butte vigilantes of 1917 who attached virtually the same message to the body of IWW organizer Frank Little after they hanged him from a railroad trestle.

In truth, Wobblies like Little were more often the victims of violence than the perpetrators; and it should be emphasized that major episodes of industrial violence in the New Northwest antedated the group by three decades. Rather than initiate a new and violent era of labor-management relations, the IWW merely elaborated on a tradition of militancy and radicalism that already existed among wageworkers of a region where sometimes turbulent labor relations owed far more to the special circumstances of life on the wageworkers' frontier than to any single organization or radical philosophy. Nonetheless,

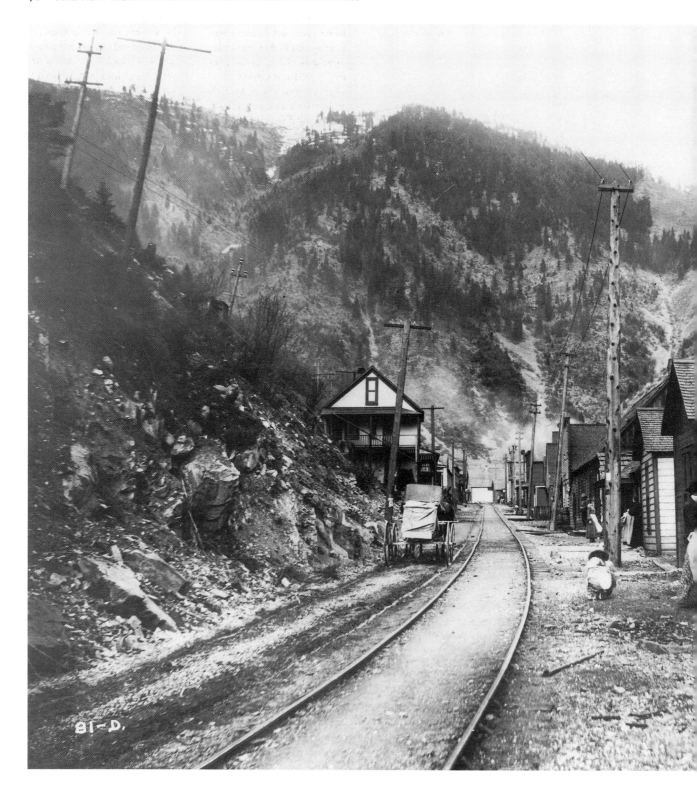

40. The environment of mining: in Idaho's lead- and silver-mining country near Wallace, the settlement of Black Bear lay at the bottom of a gulch so narrow that a single set of railway tracks doubled as the town's main street. Describing the transformation of a cold and clear northern Rocky Mountain stream after encountering this withering kind of industrial environment, the novelist Vardis Fisher, who wrote much of Idaho's Works Progress Administration guide, observed in the mid-1930s: "It has been diverted to the mines here, impregnated with poison, and turned free. It now looks like a river of lye. Or, better, it looks as if all the dirty clothes in the world had been washed in it." Fisher did not comment on what happened to humans in this environment. *Idaho, A Guide in Word and Picture* (Caldwell: Caxton Printers, 1937), 332. Courtesy Barnard-Stockbridge Collection, 8-x81d, University of Idaho Library.

Forgotten Workers: The Wives of Laboring Men

There is one class of laborers who never strike and seldom complain. They get up at five o'clock in the morning and never get back to bed until ten or eleven o'clock at night; they work without ceasing the whole of that time, and receive no other emolument than food and the plainest clothing; they understand something of every branch of economy and labor, from finance to cooking; though harassed by a thousand responsibilities, though driven and worried, though reproached and looked down upon, they never revolt, and they cannot organize for their own protection. Not even sickness releases them from their posts. No sacrifice is deemed too great for them to make, and no incompetency in any branch of their work is excused. No essays or books or poems are written to tribute their steadfastness. They die in the harness and are supplanted as quickly as may be. These are the housekeeping wives of the laboring men.

— *West Shore,* October 1886, p.307

41. The relationship between workers and bosses in the New Northwest was unintentionally emphasized in this photograph ostensibly taken to celebrate completion of the Chicago, Milwaukee & St. Paul Railway between Chicago and Seattle in 1909. Held east of Missoula, Montana, the ceremony marked the end of an era in transcontinental railroad building. Courtesy Library of Congress, no. 11604 2-62 29461.

several violent episodes together with the prominence of the IWW in the New Northwest during the decade and a half after 1905 were indications of how the labor movement both mirrored and exaggerated trends visible in other parts of the United States.

The concentration of so large a number of itinerant laborers within the region clearly influenced the course of organized labor in the New Northwest. Here, as perhaps nowhere else, the conservative, job-conscious American Federation of Labor and its affiliated craft unions faced annoying challenges from prominent advocates of alternative philosophies and organizations. Founded in 1886 as a nationwide association of craft unions under the direction of Samuel Gompers, the AF of L adopted a cautious approach that made sense in the most heavily industrialized parts of the United States. But in the New Northwest the

AF of L philosophy of organizing mainly skilled labor ignored thousands of workers in the natural resource–based industries and left them open to recruitment by alternative forms of labor organization.

Between 1890 and the First World War, many of the New Northwest's unskilled and semiskilled industrial workers believed that they had little in common with the "labor aristocrats" who belonged to the AF of L unions and to the railway brotherhoods. Consequently they continued to be drawn to industrial, inclusive, and even militant forms of labor organization like the IWW, as well as to populist, anarchist, and socialist associations and programs. Such organizations transcended occupational lines to enhance a sense of solidarity among laborers most vulnerable to exploitation and most alienated from the social mainstream.[1]

42. A charter for the Lumber Workers Industrial Union no. 120, Industrial Workers of the World. Proclaiming that "the working class and the employing class have nothing in common," the IWW called for workers in each major industry to form unions under its auspices. Together these unions would run the state. Low initiation fees and dues and easy transfer of membership between IWW unions attracted the type of casual or migratory worker so numerous in the New Northwest. Courtesy Industrial Workers of the World – Seattle Office. Records, University of Washington Libraries.

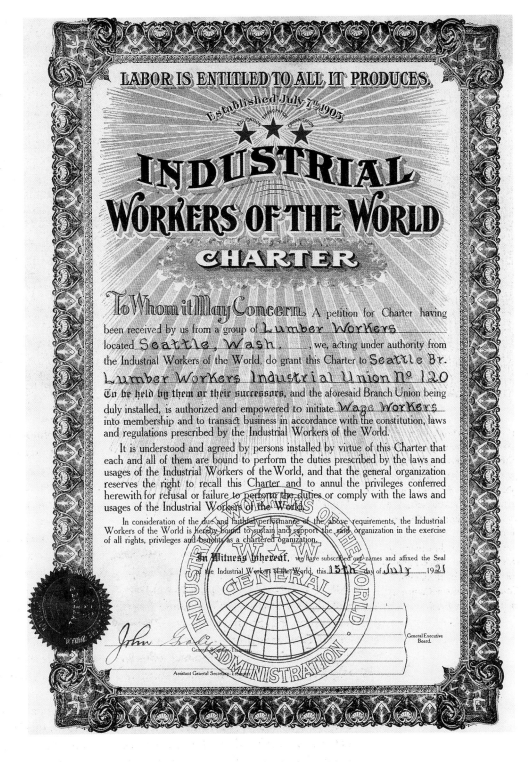

Although a handful of the New Northwest's skilled workers organized weak craft unions as early as the 1860s and 1870s, the first national labor organization to enroll many members in the nation's Far Corner was the Knights of Labor. Because Knights emphasized the solidarity of all branches of "honorable toil" – appealing to skilled and unskilled workers as well as women and blacks (but not Asians, liquor dealers, or professional gamblers) – they attracted a mass following in the New Northwest after their first local assemblies appeared there in the early 1880s. For a time the Knights of Labor emerged as a power of consequence.

Knights' assemblies combined the functions of a labor union, a fraternal lodge, a debating and educational society, and a political reform association. Elaborate and secret rituals and mysteries, created by people steeped in the rites of Free Masonry, the Odd Fellows, or Knights of Pythias, provided members with a sense of dignity, protection from the prying eyes of employers, instant community, and a welcome escape from loneliness. This idealistic but unwieldy organization was a pioneer advocate of such reforms as equal pay for men and women and elimination of child labor. The Knights encouraged workers to see themselves as members of a broadly based community of producers that constituted a true commonwealth of toil.

Promotion of labor solidarity took an ugly turn, however, during a brief but severe economic slump in the mid-1880s when Knights incited white workers to band together to boycott businesses that hired Chinese labor. Hostility to Chinese labor sprang from racism and cultural prejudice as well as from white workers' perceptions of their own economic vulnerability, and it united Caucasian workers of all nationalities against companies that used cheap, imported labor allegedly to drive down wages. Knights, who asserted that underpaid

Chinese stole jobs from white workers, played upon their fears. Caucasian workers worried that the region's new large-scale corporations would import a potentially unlimited supply of Chinese labor, thereby permanently reducing whites on the Pacific Coast to "inferiors in power and numbers." Caucasian workers believed not only that they faced formidable competitors imported from Asia, but also that they themselves represented the cutting edge of Western civilization on North America's Pacific frontier. Employers, on the other hand, often complained that they hired Chinese only when white labor was unwilling or unavailable to work.[2]

Anti-Asian hostility was not confined to organized labor, nor was it unique to the wageworkers' frontier: it was common in Australia, New Zealand, and other Caucasian-dominated parts of the Pacific Rim, but it was a distinguishing feature of western labor and served as the basis for several violent protests and third-party insurgencies. Even after the number of Chinese workers declined in the 1890s, a generalized anti-Asian hostility remained, and in the early years of the twentieth century it focused on the increasing number of Japanese workers coming to the West Coast. Not until after World War II would western labor lose its outspoken anti-Asian biases.[3]

Labor's anti-Chinese hostility first flared up in Nevada's Comstock Lode in 1869 and then evolved into a sustained crusade in San Francisco during the 1870s. It reappeared in several other areas of the West, notably in the redwood country of northern California and farther north, where Knights spearheaded a crusade to drive all Chinese labor from the New Northwest. They successfully expelled Tacoma's seven hundred Chinese merchants, gardeners, launderers, cooks, and day laborers in November 1885, but when they attempted to duplicate the feat in Seattle early the next year, they provoked a riot that led to martial

43. Union painters in the mining center of Wallace, Idaho, pose for a formal portrait. Their local, founded shortly after the turn of the century, was one of the first in Wallace to affiliate with the American Federation of Labor. Unlike the radical unions, the AF of L and its affiliates emphasized job-related goals and sought to organize only skilled workers, a minority within a regional work force that contained so many unskilled and semiskilled workers. Courtesy Barnard-Stockbridge Collection, no. 8-X330A, University of Idaho Library.

44. Chinese cannery workers either in Oregon or Washington. "There were a few small salmon canneries along the Columbia River before Chinese came to Portland in any considerable numbers. These canneries were operated with white help, but most of them failed because the laborers did not like the work and left it at the first opportunity. The large canneries were all started and have always been manned largely with Chinese laborers. This is equally true of the canneries on Puget Sound. . . . In fact, this industry has been, and still is, more dependent upon Chinese labor than any other." United States Immigration Commission, *Report,* 61st Cong., 2d Sess., 1911, SD 633, vol. 25 "Immigrants in Industries," 389. Courtesy Library of Congress, no. LC-USZ62.

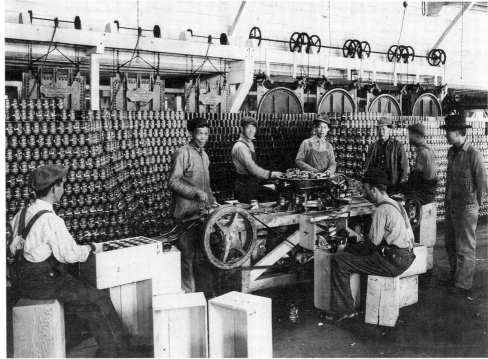

45. Seattle's anti-Chinese riot of 1886 originated as a misguided response by Caucasian workers to depression and unemployment that swept menacingly across the Pacific Northwest in the mid-1880s. Courtesy Photographic Archives, Museum of History and Industry, Seattle, no. 3130.

46. A copy of the *Four Hour Day* dating from 1912. Published in Seattle by the revolutionary socialist Dr. Hermon F. Titus and his youthful friend E. B. Ault, it set May 1, 1920, as the target date for implementation of the reform. Ault, who soon tried to best Titus by starting a publication called *The Three Hour Day for Wage Workers,* became editor of the Seattle *Union Record* in 1915. Personal publications like the *Four Hour Day* were common in the New Northwest, and they sought to address the problems of workingmen and -women, often as part of a constellation of causes such as woman suffrage, spiritualism, pacifism, free thought, single tax, direct legislation, municipal ownership, or revolutionary socialism.

The tolerant political and social atmosphere that made turn-of-the-century Washington so attractive to utopian colonists also encouraged the formation of socialist parties. Socialists came in all persuasions, from moderate "gas-and-water" types, whose main program was municipal ownership of utilities, to militant revolutionaries like Titus who called for a total overhaul of the nation's economic system. Moderate socialists were occasionally victorious at the polls, and they served in a variety of posts, among them, city commissioner of Spokane, mayor of Pasco, and member of the state House of Representatives. Socialists also scored victories in Anaconda and Butte, Montana, where they elected a mayor in 1911. Courtesy Harry Ault Papers, University of Washington Libraries.

The Culture of Labor

Assemblies of the Knights of Labor functioned as social and educational agencies in the New Northwest. Their frequent entertainment programs were well attended. To the Knights' 1886 picnic and clambake on Alki Point came more than two thousand men and women from Seattle and several hundred more from Tacoma, Black Diamond, Newcastle, and Renton. The former territorial governor William Newell addressed the gathering. Two years later the Knights organized Seattle's first Labor Day celebration, a festive occasion complete with racing contests, band music, and speeches – many speeches. Dancing the evening away at a Knights of Labor grand ball was another popular form of worker entertainment.

The typical Knights of Labor social was a high-minded affair, a mixture of instructive oratory, poetic recitations, instrumental solos, and, occasionally, orchestral music. While most of the music was valued solely as entertainment, the Knights sometimes combined sarcastic comments with the well-known melodies of religious and patriotic hymns to create a form of propaganda in song. The words from a typical piece, sung to the tune of "America," indicate how cynically the Knights regarded public life in the early 1890s:

> Our Country, 'tis of thee,
> Sweet land of knavery,
>   Of thee we sing!
> Sweet land of Jobs and Rings,
> And various crooked things –
> Our social system brings
>   Full many a sting.

Probably no labor organization ever used protest music more effectively than the Industrial Workers of the World. "It is really surprising," said a Spokane Wobbly, "how soon a crowd will form on the street to hear a song in the interest of the working class, familiar as they are with the maudlin sentimental music of various religionists." Published in the famous little red songbook that the IWW began issuing in 1909, songs like "Hallelujah, I'm a Bum," "The Rebel Girl," "Dump the Bosses off Your Back" – the latter sung to the tune of "Take It to The Lord in Prayer" – and "Commonwealth of Toil" were used to fan "the holy flame of discontent." – Adapted from Carlos A. Schwantes, "Churches of the Disinherited: The Culture of Radicalism on the North Pacific Industrial Frontier," *Pacific Historian* 25 (Winter 1981), 54–65

law and use of federal troops to quell the disorder.[4]

Violence, both in the Pacific Northwest and elsewhere contributed to the Knights' undoing. Membership dropped, and the organization largely disappeared from the New Northwest by the turn of the century. Even so, the Knights left an important legacy. As the dominant labor organization during the formative decade of the 1880s, it probably did more to shape the region's early labor culture than any other group. Local trade unionists as well as populists, socialists, anarchists, communitarians on Puget Sound, and members of the Industrial Workers of the World were all to some degree influenced by the Knights of Labor.

Disillusioned by the violence of the mid-1880s, some former Seattle Knights concluded that industrial society could be reformed only by creation of a workable alternative. They organized a model commonwealth called the Puget Sound Co-Operative Colony near Port Angeles. It was the first of several utopian experiments located on Puget Sound. Additional

47. Washington's First Socialist Encampment at Olalla in 1915. The state's radical culture dated back to the mid-1880s when people distressed by the apparent failings of the new industrial society founded the Puget Sound Co-Operative Colony near Port Angeles. This was the first of several utopian experiments on Puget Sound, some of which attracted recruits from all over the nation. In 1897, when trains brought thousands of gold seekers to Seattle, where they boarded ships headed north to the fabulous Klondike diggings, they occasionally carried passengers of another sort, dreamers who sought neither gold nor glory but only a chance to build a brave new world in the wilds of Washington. The availability of so much fertile land on Puget Sound at a time when the ideas of Henry George, Edward Bellamy, and the socialist thinkers were gaining popularity seemed to present reformers one last opportunity to break out of the dehumanizing industrial system that was so much a feature of life in the commercial and manufacturing centers of the eastern United States and Europe.

Utopias, bearing such quaint names as Home, Equality, and Freeland, arose on Puget Sound's isolated bays and tidal flats. The hope of many was to transform Washington into a model commonwealth, a workable alternative to the larger society that seemed to suffer more social tension and economic dislocation with each passing year. Courtesy Forest History Society.

"OLD FRIENDS REUNITED" AT WASHINGTON'S FIRST SOCIALIST ENCAMPMENT. OLALLA   JULY 3, 4, 5.   1915

ones originated during the depression years of the 1890s. Most of them were socialist, but Home Colony, located across the sound from Tacoma, was anarchist and attracted a measure of infamy across the state when some members insisted on swimming nude.[5]

Other Knights turned to political reform. After their failure to expel Seattle's Chinese, they sought change through the ballot box. In the fall of 1886, the Knights organized the Territorial People's party and persuaded the former Washington governor William Newell to run as the party's delegate to Congress. The party proved a failure, but its twenty-six-plank reform platform endured. When the Knights of Labor spearheaded the formation of a new third party in 1891 – the People's or Populist party, which soon evolved into a major influence in the young state – the 1886 platform was its foundation.[6]

There were also former Knights who helped organize craft unions in the New Northwest for the recently formed American Federation of Labor. They looked back upon their participation in the anti-Chinese violence with regret and were determined not to waste time trying to organize both skilled and unskilled workers, or workers by industry; rather, they would keep the AF of L focused on organizing only the skilled workers in specific trades and on seeking "bread-and-butter gains" like higher wages and longer hours.

Yet even as Gompers and the AF of L sought to organize the skilled workers of the West, the peculiarities of the region left its mark on the union. Pressure from its members in the West led the American Federation to adopt an anti-Chinese stance. The AF of L also had to contend with the sense of westernness that in some of its own members manifested itself in a desire

48. Main street on the irrigation frontier. At the time of its Labor Day parade in 1906, Twin Falls, Idaho, was barely two years old. Despite the impression created by this picture, organized labor was not strong there. Labor unions, in fact, found that organizing workers of the New Northwest was seldom easy, and they never attracted a majority of the region's wageworkers, even in Washington, which at various times was the most highly unionized state in the country. Neither was labor's influence uniform throughout the region. Its chief centers of strength were the mining towns of the interior, places like Butte and the camps of Idaho's Coeur d'Alene district, and the seaports of Seattle and Tacoma. Labor's power was especially low in southern Idaho, which apart from Boise and Pocatello had few urban areas and little manufacturing. Courtesy Idaho State Historical Society, no.73-221.799.

TWIN FALLS ON LABOR DAY, 1906.
BISBEE PHOTO-812.

to avoid domination by leaders from outside the region. A sense of westernness could work to the disadvantage of national unions headquartered in the East by creating friction and in some instances by provoking outright rebellion that resulted in the formation of new western unions. The twentieth century saw celebrated splits between East and West in the longshoremen's and papermakers' unions, among others.[7]

Another noticeable characteristic of western labor was its affinity for industrial forms of union organization. Because of the large number of workers employed in labor-intensive industries that dominated the regional economy, industrial unions tended to be popular even among local affiliates of the American Federation of Labor. Long after the AF of L established its hegemony over most western unions in the early years of the twentieth century, sup-

Abandoning the "Land of Dreams"

In 1887 there began an invasion of this district by the organizations belonging to the American Federation of Labor. . . . We began to learn what the organization of labor really meant. We ceased to some extent at least to live in the land of dreams and faced realities. We began to struggle for economic necessities, the reduction of hours, increase of wages and other conditions of employment. The trade unions grew as rapidly as the Knights of Labor declined over the entire Northwest. – C. O. ("Dad") Young, AF of L organizer, and former member of the Knights of Labor on Puget Sound, in *Yearbook of Organized Labor of the State of Washington*, 1930 (n.p., [1931]), 18

49. A Wobbly picnic in Seattle in 1919. Members are holding up copies of various labor newspapers including the *Industrial Worker*, first issued in Spokane in 1909 and one of the region's most famous labor publications. This well-dressed gathering was probably intended as a fund raiser, an important social occasion for radicals in the New Northwest. At one such, a ball in Tacoma, anarchists rented a hall and invited friends to enjoy an elaborate mixture of oratory, music, and games. Musical selections were performed by vocalists, pianists, "Prof. Jensen's full orchestra," and the Tacoma Zither Club. A popular game was "grape picking," in which comrades attempted to steal certain objects without getting caught and fined. One player acted as jailer, and the "slickest thief" got a prize. Courtesy Special Collections Division, University of Washington Libraries, UW no.6633.

port for industrial unionism remained a matter of contention between the AF of L's national leadership and industrial-minded unionists in the West. At the AF of L's national conventions, affiliates from the New Northwest could usually be counted on to support the industrial union resolutions that were regularly introduced between 1901 and World War I.

For a brief time in the late 1890s and early 1900s, unions affiliated with the American Federation of Labor dominated labor affairs in the New Northwest. Indeed, at the AF of L's national convention in 1892, President Gompers was able to report that the threat of rival labor organizations on the Pacific Coast had ended because the "previously isolated" unions there had "entered into fraternal bonds with those in the East." Yet despite his optimism, alternative forms of labor organization in the New Northwest did not really die with the Knights of Labor. First to pick up where the Knights left off were the metal miners of Idaho's Coeur d'Alene district, who conceived the idea of a new regionwide union of miners and smelter workers following the violence of 1892. Many northern Idaho miners wintered in Spokane, the last stronghold of the Knights of Labor in Washington, and had became familiar with the Knights' program through the organization's lyceums and its local newspaper, the *Freemen's Labor Journal*. Although the Western Federation of Miners, which was born in the 1892 Coeur d'Alene violence and formally established in Butte in 1893, affiliated briefly with the AF of L, it broke ranks later in the decade and opposed the American Federation as little more than an instrument of colonial domination.[8]

The miners' organization also served as a bridge between the Knights of Labor and the Industrial Workers of the World, which metal miners helped to organize in Chicago in 1905. Although they did not limit their activities to the West, members of the IWW seemed more at

Learning Labor History

Pat was the oldest man on the job, tall, raw-boned, with a red chin-whisker, bushy eyebrows and a strawberry mark on the outer corner of his left eye. It was this old Irishman who gave me my first lessons in unionism. Pat was a member of the Knights of Labor, and some of the things he told me about this organization I could not well understand at the time. I had never heard of the need of workingmen organizing for mutual protection. In that part of the country there did not seem to be a wide division between the boss and the men. The old man who was the boss slept in the same room and ate at the same table and appeared the same as the rest of the men. But Pat explained that he was not the real boss; that none of us knew the owner of the mine. Mentioning the large ranches in the vicinity, he said, "The owners live in California, while the men who do all the work and make the ranches of value are here in Nevada." He told me about the unions he had belonged to, the miners' union in Bodie, California, and the Virginia City Miners' Union in Nevada, organized in 1867, the first miners' union in America. These two unions were among the first that formed the Western Federation of Miners. — William D. Haywood, *Bill Haywood's Book* (New York: International Publishers, 1929), 30–31

home on the wageworkers' frontier than anywhere else in the United States. Their program was clearly tailored to meet the needs of laborers in the New Northwest, and especially those workers most alienated from the mainstream of society by the brutal working and living conditions they encountered in camps and mills. At a time when nationally oriented trade unions concentrated their efforts on skilled labor, Wobblies emphasized the solidarity of all

workers – men and women, whites and blacks, even the Asians shunned by Knights. The IWW kept dues low and ignored political action since workers seldom remained in one place long enough to qualify to vote. Wobblies also refused to sign contracts with employers, whom they regarded as mortal enemies.[9]

By having to confront some of the roughest and most arbitrary working conditions in the United States, the IWW came to exhibit a strain of militancy that was seemingly a natural by-product of the western laborers' struggle for existence. It was these conditions that gave radical unions like the Industrial Workers of the World a prominence in the West seldom attained elsewhere in the nation. Workers were drawn by Wobblies' militant radicalism expressed in colorful protest songs and unorthodox organizing tactics. In this way the IWW attracted wageworkers who cared nothing for

The Spirit of the IWW

The nomadic worker of the West embodies the very spirit of the IWW . . . His anomalous position, half industrial slave, half vagabond adventurer, leaves him infinitely less servile than his fellow worker in the East. Unlike the factory slave of the Atlantic seaboard and the Central States he is most emphatically not "afraid of his job." His mobility is amazing. Buoyantly confident of his ability to "get by" somehow, he promptly shakes the dust of a locality from his feet whenever the board is bad, or the boss too exacting, or the work unduly tiresome, departing for the next job, even if it be 500 miles away. Cost of transportation does not daunt him. "Freight trains run every day," and his ingenuity is a match for the vigilance of trainmen and special police. No wife or family cumber him. The workman of the East, oppressed by the fear of want for wife and babies, dares not venture much. He has perforce the tameness of the domesticated animals. — *Solidarity*, Nov. 21, 1914, quoted in Cloice Ray Howd, *Industrial Relations in the West Coast Lumber Industry* (Washington, DC: GPO, 1924), 54

The Rebel Girl

When I came to Spokane in December 1909 the all-male committee was somewhat disconcerted to be told that I was pregnant. They decided that I was not to speak on the forbidden streets but confine myself to speaking in the IWW halls, to clubs and organizations willing to give us a hearing, and in nearby places to raise defense funds. I made trips to Seattle, British Columbia, Idaho and Montana. A few months later after five editors of the *Industrial Worker* had been arrested and it was harder for me to travel, I was put in charge of the paper. I felt fine, but my co-workers were disturbed about having me appear in public. In those days pregnant women usually concealed themselves from public view. "It don't look nice. Besides, Gurley'll have that baby right on the platform if she's not careful!" one fussy old guy protested. One night on my way to the IWW hall, I was arrested, charged with "conspiracy to incite men to violate the law," and lodged in the county jail. I was only in jail one night and was released the next day on bail, put up by a prominent club woman.

There had been such an orgy of police brutality in Spokane that my friends back East were greatly concerned. I struck the Spokane authorities a real blow, however, by describing in the next issue of the *Industrial Worker* my overnight experiences in the county jail. The entire edition of the paper was confiscated and suppressed. But the story went all over the country and hundreds of protests poured in. I took my story to the local Women's Club, and they demanded a matron be placed in the jail. — Elizabeth Gurley Flynn, *The Rebel Girl* rev. ed. (New York: International Publishers, 1973), 108–9

50. Holding the fort in Everett. The words on the banner come from the title of one of labor's popular anthems:

Hold the fort for we are coming –
Union men, be strong.
Side by side we battle onward,
Victory will come.

"Hold the Fort" originated as a gospel song written in 1870, was popular among Knights of Labor, and entered the Wobblies' little red songbook in 1914. Courtesy Archives of Labor and Urban Affairs, Wayne State University.

– or did not even pretend to understand – its syndicalist ideology.[10]

Wobblies gained attention slowly after their founding in Chicago, then burst into newspaper headlines in 1909 when they launched a spectacular and unorthodox protest called a "free speech fight," a demonstration designed to call attention to the exploitation of harvest labor in the inland Northwest. For defying Spokane's ban on street-corner speaking, hundreds of Wobblies – some of whom had only recited the Declaration of Independence – were arrested and jailed. "In the Spokane jails they perfected their technique of the 'battle-ship,' which sends all prisoners on a noise-making spree at a given signal, producing a din that would test the walls of Jericho." Nearly every inbound train brought more Wobblies to Spokane to speak until the city, faced with a lack of jail space, mounting expenses, and bad publicity, declined to pursue the struggle; it soon outlawed the dishonest employment agencies the IWW so detested.[11]

Wobblies considered the free speech fight a success and employed the technique wherever they had a grievance to dramatize. Free speech fights gave them a reputation for defiance that aroused the deepest anxieties of many ob-

MEMORIAL SERVICES HELD AT MT. PLEASANT CEMETERY FOR THE EVERETT VICTIMS MAY-1-1917

51. Everett Memorial on May Day 1917. When the oppressive tactics of Everett employers clashed with IWW assertiveness, the result was tragedy. A free speech fight began when Wobblies intervened in a strike initiated earlier by shingle weavers affiliated with the American Federation of Labor. In response, local deputies beat Wobblies and expelled them from town. Hoping to avoid the lawmen who patrolled the highways and rail lines into Everett, more than two hundred Wobblies sailed north from Seattle on the steamship *Verona* on November 5, 1916. A gun-toting force of deputies awaited them on the Everett dock. Shots rang out – from where was never proven – and when the firing stopped moments later, five Wobblies and two deputies lay dying. Several panicked Wobblies jumped overboard and apparently drowned; a total of fifty men on both sides were wounded. In the ensuing trial in Seattle of the first seventy-four Wobblies charged with first-degree murder, the attorney George Vanderveer, the self-described "counsel for the damned," won an acquittal. Everett was the Wobblies' last major free speech fight. Courtesy Archives of Labor and Urban Affairs, Wayne State University.

52. Members of the Spruce Production Division near Lake Crescent, Washington. Troops were also stationed at various locations along the Oregon coast, such as Toledo, where fifteen hundred of them cut spruce for a giant new plant designed to supply lumber for aircraft construction. Courtesy Washington State Historical Society, A. Curtis no. 38414.

servers and made the union vulnerable to vigilantism and other forms of repressive action. The unusual tactics of IWW members, their radicalism and contempt for authority, and their vulnerablity to persecution as community outsiders led to several violent and celebrated clashes with employers and lawmen. Free speech fights eventually spread to Vancouver, British Columbia, and about twenty-five other western communities, but in Everett, Washington, in November 1916, a confrontation ended in a major tragedy.

Wobblies were conducting their most successful strike in the Northwest's lumber industry when America joined the First World War in April 1917. Their protest – which included the classic on-the-job slowdown – cut production to 15 percent of normal and drove the industry to its knees before changed circum-stances gave it a powerful new ally in Uncle Sam. The number of strikes in the region's lumber industry had soared from 44 in 1916 to 295 in 1917, severely hampering production for war. Because the lumber industry convinced the federal government that spruce, a light strong wood used in aircraft construction, was vital to the war effort, Uncle Sam was in no mood to tolerate a strike. The government's response to the Wobbly slowdown was a two-fisted attack: creation of a military organization, the Spruce Production Division, which put twenty-seven thousand soldiers to work in the lumber camps, and a quasi–company union, the Loyal Legion of Loggers and Lumbermen (4-L's). Formed during the summer of 1917, the Loyal Legion gained about one hundred thousand members who signed a patriotic pledge not to strike.[12]

53. Special Centralia edition of the IWW songbook (1925). On November 11, 1919, members of the newly formed American Legion staged a parade in Centralia, Washington, to celebrate the first anniversary of the end of World War I. The parade route wound past the IWW Hall, where some marchers broke ranks and charged toward the building. Shots rang out. Who fired first remains unknown, for both sides were armed, but in a confusing few seconds, four legionnaires fell to the ground, mortally wounded. That night vigilantes terrorized Wobbly prisoners held in the local jail and seized Wesley Everest, a United States Army veteran, and hanged him from a nearby railroad bridge. After a celebrated trial, a court convicted eight Wobblies of second-degree murder for the parade deaths and sentenced them to lengthy prison terms. The last of the jailed Wobblies was not released until 1939. No one was ever charged with the murder of Everest.

Apart from encouraging federal officials to improve working and living conditions in the woods and frightening employers into bargaining with less radical labor unions, the IWW left a colorful legacy of protest songs and demonstrations. Today that legacy is part of the legend and folklore celebrating the robust life-style so typical of earning a living in the New Northwest. Courtesy Industrial Workers of the World – Seattle Office. *Records,* University of Washington Libraries.

Together these two organizations provided spruce and other lumber for the war effort. Membership in the Industrial Workers of the World declined precipitously, not only because of the Spruce Production Division and the 4-L's but also because of federal raids and vigilante attacks on its meeting halls and leaders. Ironically, the presence of Uncle Sam's troops in the lumber camps mandated many improvements that Wobblies had long sought, such as the eight-hour day, shower facilities, and clean bunkhouses. A case can be made that the decline of the Wobblies after 1917 was a direct result of government repression, but coupled with that repression were federally sponsored improvements in living and working conditions in the lumber camps, that for all practical purposes undercut the Wobblies' raison d'être. Perhaps having the greatest impact on Wobbly fortunes was the disappearance of the wageworkers' frontier.[13]

The closing of the wageworkers' frontier did not occur at a specific time, nor was it unusually dramatic. It would be a mistake to argue that the wageworkers' frontier existed much past World War I, yet vestiges of it certainly lingered in the forests and mines of the West, perhaps as late as World War II. In some locales the end came when the coal or ore ran out or when the land was logged off. A drop in the price of copper or silver and the competition that California oil brought to the coal mines of the New Northwest also contributed to the demise. The end also came when one-time frontier communities achieved a measure of economic and social maturity and when a new generation of workers apparently resigned themselves to a life of working for wages. Changing technology played a role too by thinning the ranks of itinerant laborers.

When electricity came to north Idaho during the 1890s, for instance, it became possible to operate the metal mines year-round instead of shutting down when winter weather froze

Last Hurrah

As the depression deepened in 1921, the 9- and 10-hour day crept back into the logging camps and with it many of the old evils of bad food and lodging. In 1923 the Wobblies rallied for their final general strike in the woods for the eight-hour day. Using all the old techniques which had served so well in 1917, the strike failed to become general. Lumber Workers Industrial Union 500 was finished in the camps.
– Harvey O'Connor, *Revolution in Seattle* (1964; rpt. Seattle: Left Bank Books, 1981), 212

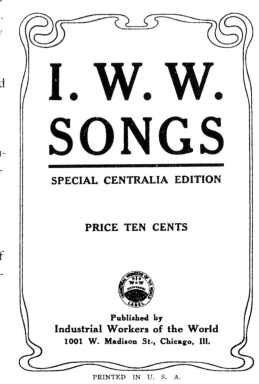

I. W. W.
SONGS

SPECIAL CENTRALIA EDITION

PRICE TEN CENTS

Published by
Industrial Workers of the World
1001 W. Madison St., Chicago, Ill.

PRINTED IN U. S. A.

54. A stationary threshing machine at work at an unspecified location in Oregon in the early twentieth century. Straw was used for fuel in the steam engine; water came from a nearby creek. The derrick team used a net to unload the cut grain from a "header bed." Men used pitchforks to feed the separator or threshing machine.

The Supreme Court justice William O. Douglas recalled an unsettling incident that occurred while he worked with a similar crew in eastern Washington: "The most interesting encounter I ever had with a rattlesnake happened when I worked in the wheat fields with Blacky. The separator would blow out the chaff, and we used it to make a pile about four feet high and long and broad enough for two bedrolls. When Blacky and I put our bedrolls down and got inside them, the chaff would settle into a rather thin but comfortable mattress. One bright moonlit night I was wakened out of a sound sleep by a blood-curdling scream from Blacky. I sat up and saw him somewhere in the air between me and the moon. When he came down, he did not stop running until he reached the header-box. Only when he was safe did he explain what happened. In language unfit to quote he said that a rattler had crawled in bed with him and wrapped itself around his feet.

"'He was just trying to get warm,' I shouted.

"Blacky's reply is not fit for print, either. Thereafter he never, never slept on the ground." *Go East, Young Man* (New York: Random House, 1974), 75. Courtesy Oregon Historical Society, no.6176, file 10-A.

the water that generated the power. During the years after the First World War, the growing number of gasoline-powered mechanical harvesters and the shipment of wheat to market in bulk rather than in individual burlap sacks dramatically reduced the need for harvest hands on the bonanza grain ranches, often by as much as two-thirds or more.[14]

Steam shovels displaced many of the common laborers who constructed and maintained railway lines and irrigation ditches. The nation's rail mileage peaked in 1916, and within a few years, railroad construction camps populated by transient single males had largely become relics of the past. World War I brought other significant changes too. Improved living and working conditions in the logging industry during and after the war helped make it possible for loggers to marry and settle down outside the camps. Where efforts were made to create some kind of true community in the camps, it tended to "decasualize" the lumberjack. The availability of cheap used cars and all-weather highways also contributed to the demise of the wageworkers' frontier. Instead of "riding the rods," many migratory laborers now followed the harvest in their own second-hand automobiles, and loggers in increasing numbers drove to work from towns and villages located outside the camps. For some, "automobility" became the equivalent of upward social mobility.

Impact of the Motor Truck

Sawmills usually are found in, or near, permanent settlements, although there are many exceptions in the case of small mills. In recent years the motor truck literally has been pulling the small mill out of the woods. Many sawmill communities, however, are comprised of only the lumber company's employees and are frequently quite isolated. – Vernon H. Jensen, *Lumber and Labor* (New York: Farrar & Rinehart, 1945), 12

55. Harvesting wheat in Walla Walla County, Washington, July 1941; by this time, grain was shipped in bulk and modern machinery had dramatically reduced the need for itinerant labor. The agricultural historian Alexander C. McGregor assessed the changes that tractors brought to his family's ranch in eastern Washington during the 1920s: "The 1929 crop year was the last time the McGregors would use large crews of traveling harvest hands. The sailors, miners, Canadian farmers, 'hoboes,' 'card sharks,' and various other trained horse and mule skinners were no longer necessary." By 1970, observed McGregor, seven men, equipped with three self-propelled, air-conditioned combines, a "bankout wagon" to haul the wheat from combines to trucks waiting at the edge of the fields, and three trucks handled harvest operations that once required a hundred men and 310 horses and mules. *Counting Sheep: From Open Range to Agribusiness on the Columbia Plateau* (Seattle: University of Washington Press, 1982), 270, 314. Courtesy Library of Congress, no.15-761 LC-USF 34 39914.

Organizers for the Industrial Workers of the World complained that as a result of automobile ownership fracturing the work force, it became increasingly difficult to recruit itinerant laborers. The sense of worker solidarity that knew no occupational boundaries diminished and disappeared along with the migratory life-style. As individual wageworkers got married and established homes, they usually developed attitudes more accommodating to the social and economic system. This evolution in life-styles tended to undermine any previous commitment to fundamental change.[15]

Migratory laborers – so visible in the Pacific Northwest's extractive industries – did not disappear with the close of the wageworkers' frontier, although after 1920 they were increasingly confined to agriculture. Mechanization of the grain harvest greatly reduced the need for laborers, but the harvest of fruit, vegetables, berries, sugar beets, hops, and other crops still required enormous numbers of seasonal workers. In the 1930s the migrants who followed the crops were predominantly "white-American" families, many of them recent arrivals from the drought- and depression-stricken Great Plains. Thousands of them came in search of the Northwest's fabled "pastures of plenty." During 1936 alone, an estimated ten thousand farm families fled the northern plains for Washington, Oregon, Idaho, and western Montana. They hoped to establish permanent homes, perhaps on cutover timberlands, but many ended up working as seasonal laborers, supplanting the single, male harvest hands of earlier years. The composition of the work force continued to evolve with the growing number of Hispanics in the region's fields and orchards, especially as a result of severe labor shortages during World War II.[16]

Despite the changes in its work force and in working and living conditions, the Pacific Northwest in the interwar years remained economically what it had been for much of the previous century: a producer of raw and semifinished materials. To be sure, Oregon surpassed Washington as the nation's number one timber producer in 1938, but that did not alter the fact that both states, together with Idaho and Montana, were economically dependent on natural resource-based industries vulnerable to the Great Depression. About half of Idaho's population in 1930 depended directly on agriculture for a living, about one-tenth relied on manufacturing – mostly timber – and a much smaller portion on mining. Agrarian Idaho had never shared the prosperity of the 1920s, but the disastrous economic decline of the early 1930s made the previous years seem almost prosperous by comparison. In Oregon the economic collapse brought 90 percent of the timber companies to the verge of bankruptcy, and at least half of the state's timberlands were tax delinquent. Huge federally supported building projects like Bonneville and Grand Coulee dams sustained many of the newly jobless. For a time it appeared that the wageworkers' frontier had reappeared in updated form in construction boomtowns like Grand Coulee, Washington.[17]

The 1930s were an especially stormy time of strikes and schism in the house of labor. The ranks of organized workers expanded rapidly as a result of federal prolabor legislation, but the nearly uncontrolled growth worsened friction between advocates of craft and industrial unions. When the American Federation of Labor expelled proponents of industrial unionism in 1937, they formed the Congress of Industrial Organizations (CIO) the following year. The labor rivalry was especially bitter in the Pacific Northwest, where the aggressive CIO in some ways embodied both the fiery militancy of the Industrial Workers of the World and the idealism of the Knights of Labor. The CIO's strength in the region lay in the timber and mining industries, in the fish canneries,

56. Linemen working near Moscow, Idaho, were harbingers of a new age of electricity that would profoundly change both home and factory. Electric motors replaced steam-driven overhead shafts and belts to power all kinds of industrial equipment. Courtesy Washington Water Power Company.

and on the waterfront. The International Woodworkers of America, formed in 1937, battled for the CIO in the Northwest's woods and mills. Membership in the craft-oriented AF of L was less concentrated, but under the leadership of Dave Beck, a fast-rising star in the Teamsters' Union, it vigorously opposed the CIO. By the eve of World War II when workers were suddenly in short supply, both the strikes and labor's internecine warfare diminished.[18]

The Second World War inaugurated the modern era of Pacific Northwest history by expanding the range of employment opportunities well beyond the basic ones that had prevailed since the days of the wageworkers' frontier. Although no region of the United States escaped the impact of war, few if any experienced more rapid and intense changes than the Pacific Northwest. Wartime social and economic pressures scarcely left a corner untouched. Even before the United States formally declared war on the Axis nations of Japan, Germany, and Italy in December 1941, the Pacific Northwest had increased production for defense and for aid to friendly nations already at war. The surprise Japanese attack on Pearl Harbor rapidly accelerated that trend. Industries large and small produced ships, barges, aircraft, lumber and various kinds of wood products, metals, food, machinery, clothing, munitions, and armaments. The region's two best-known war industries were the Kaiser Company shipyards in the Portland-Vancouver area and the Boeing Airplane Company. Seattle alone secured war contracts totaling $5.6 billion, ranking it among the nation's top three cities in per capita war orders. At its peak of production in 1944, Boeing employed nearly fifty thousand people in the Seattle area and amassed total sales of more than $600 million, an impressive sum considering that in 1939 the value of all Seattle manufacturing totaled only $70 million.[19]

57. Fruits of electrification: a short course in household electrical equipment held in 1929 at Oregon State College. Vacuum cleaners and irons were the most popular items in the typical home. After World War I most advertisements that aimed at women depicted housewives doing their own domestic chores and virtually eliminated pictures of servants. Courtesy Oregon State University Archives, no.978.

As they had during the era of the wage-workers' frontier, professional Northwest photographers continued to document regional work life. Few of them, however, still produced images for promotional literature. Pamphlets issued by railroads and chambers of commerce declined both in number and variety after 1920, and most were less lavishly illustrated than they had been two decades earlier. During the lean years of the 1930s and again during World War II, the best scenes of Northwest work life were often those captured on film by government photographers, men and

women hired by the Farm Security Administration and other federal agencies. Their images tended to serve as public relations tools for the New Deal and later wartime programs.[20]

Like the promotional pictures from earlier decades, federal photographs idealized some aspects of work and failed to capture others, yet collectively they make visible the rich heritage of workers in the Pacific Northwest. The following folios seek to gather the best of those images to document informally one region's work life from the 1880s through the 1940s.

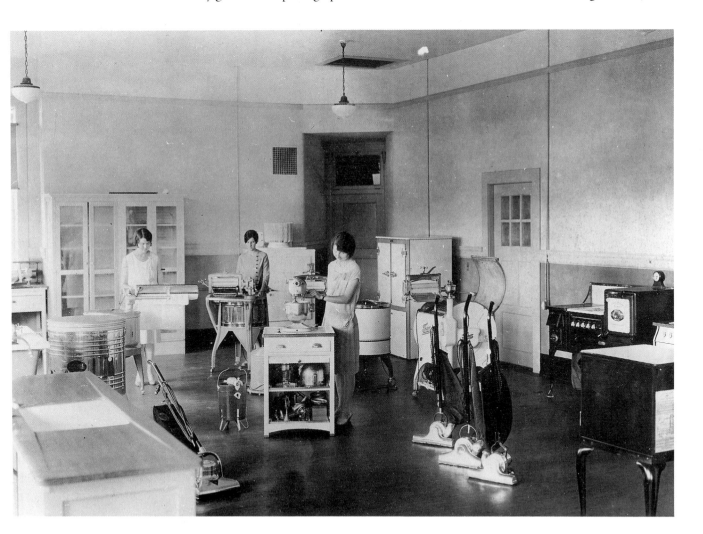

58. A streetcar and automobile col-
lided on the crowded streets of
Spokane in 1929. This type of photograph was taken mainly for insurance purposes and, unless it
appeared in a newspaper, was never
seen by the public. It illustrates how
certain photographs of life in the
Pacific Northwest failed to enter the
region's historical consciousness.
Courtesy Eastern Washington State
Historical Society, no.L86-
588.207.

Notes

Preface

1. One indication of growing awareness of labor's contribution to the general history of the American West is Richard White, *"It's Your Misfortune and None of My Own": A New History of the American West* (Norman: University of Oklahoma Press, 1991). See especially pages 277–97, which provide an exceptionally fine summary of the topic.

2. *Idaho, A Guide in Word and Picture.* See Federal Writers' Project, Works Progress (and Projects) Administration, publications: (Caldwell, Idaho: Caxton Printers, 1937); *Montana, A State Guide Book* (New York: Viking Press, 1939); *Oregon, End of the Trail* (Portland: Binfords & Mort, 1940); and *Washington, A Guide to the Evergreen State* (Portland: Binfords & Mort, 1941). United States Immigration Commission, *Report,* 61st Cong., 2d Sess., 1911, SD 633, vol.25, "Immigrants in Industries"; Richard L. Neuberger, *Our Promised Land* (New York: Macmillan, 1938). A professional journalist, Neuberger represented Oregon in the U.S. Senate from 1955 to 1960.

3. Graham Adams, Jr., *The Age of Industrial Violence, 1910–1915: The Activities and Findings of the United States Industrial Commission* (New York: Columbia University Press, 1966), 50. *Report of the Commission on Industrial Relations,* 11 vols., 64th Cong., 1st Sess., 1916, Senate Document 415.

Chapter 1

1. This description of the final spike ceremonies is derived from Carlos A. Schwantes, *Railroad Signatures across the Pacific Northwest* (Seattle: University of Washington Press, 1993), 57–60.

2. Ray Stannard Baker, "Destiny and the Western Railroad," *Century Magazine* 75 (April 1908), 892–94. See also *idem,* "The Great Northwest," *Century Magazine* 65 (March 1903), 647–67. On railroad promotion of the New Northwest, see Schwantes, *Railroad Signatures across the Pacific Northwest,* especially the chapters titled "Shapers of a New Northwest" and "Twentieth-Century Empire Builders."

3. "The Pacific Northwest Advertising Campaign, 1923." Copy in Northern Pacific Papers, 10-B-11-5, Minnesota Historical Society, St. Paul.

4. Edward W. Nolan, *Northern Pacific Views: The Rail-road Photography of F. Jay Haynes, 1876–1905* (Helena: Montana Historical Society Press, 1983).

5. Alan Trachtenberg, *Reading American Photographs: Images as History, Mathew Brady to Walker Evans* (New York City: Hill and Wang, 1989), 164–230 *passim.*

6. Dennis A. Andersen, "Clark Kinsey: Logging Photography, 1914–1945," *Pacific Northwest Quarterly* 74 (1983), 18–27; Dave Bohn and Rodolfo Petschek, *Kinsey Photographer: A Half Century of Negatives by Darius and Tabitha May Kinsey* (San Francisco: Chronicle Books, 1982); Mark H. Brown and W. R. Felton: *The Frontier Years: L. A. Huffman, Photographer of the Plains* (New York: Henry Holt & Co., 1955); Richard Frederick and Jeanne Engerman, *Asahel Curtis: Photographs of the Great Northwest* (Tacoma: Washington State Historical Society, 1983); Patricia Hart and Ivar Nelson, *Mining Town: The Photographic Record of T. N. Barnard and Nellie Stockbridge from the Coeur d'Alenes* (Seattle: University of Washington Press, 1984); Donna M. Lucey, *Photographing Montana, 1894–1928: The Life and Work of Evelyn Cameron* (New York: Alfred A. Knopf, 1990); Glenn Mason, "The Libby Collection of Spokane, Washington," *Journal of the West* 28 (January 1989), 59–65; Peter Palmquist, ed., "Photography in the West," *Journal of the West* 25 (April 1987), and 28 (January 1989), two special issues devoted to western photography; JoAnn Roe, *Frank Matsura: Frontier Photographer* (Seattle: Madrona Publishers, 1981); Robert A. Weinstein, *Grays Harbor, 1885–1913* (New York: Viking Press, 1978), which utilized the photography of Charles Pratsch; Robert A. Weinstein, *Tall Ships on Puget Sound: The Marine Photographs of Wilhelm Hester* (Seattle: University of Washington Press, 1978). See also *Union Guide to Photograph Collections in the Pacific Northwest* (Portland: Oregon Historical Society, 1978).

7. In addition to the Frederick and Engerman book on Curtis, see Archie Satterfield, *Seattle: An Asahel Curtis Portfolio* (San Francisco: Chronicle Books, 1985). Of Asahel Curtis's 60,000 negatives, about half survive today.

8. *Images of America: A Panorama of History in Photographs* (Washington, D.C.: Smithsonian Books,

1989); Martin W. Sandler, *American Image: Photographing One Hundred Fifty Years in the Life of the Nation* (Chicago: Contemporary Books, 1989); Martha A. Sandweiss, ed., *Photography in Nineteenth-Century America* (Fort Worth: Amon Carter Museum, 1991). See also Pete Daniel, Merry A. Foresta, Maren Stange, and Sally Stein, *Official Images: New Deal Photography* (Washington, D.C.: Smithsonian Institution Press, 1987).

9. Lee Moorhouse, *Souvenir Album of Noted Indian Photographs* (Pendleton, Oreg.: East Oregonian Printing, 1905).

10. A representative sampling of books and articles that study different categories of western workers is included in the For Further Reading section. Probably the most important essay on western workers as a group is Melvyn Dubofsky, "The Origins of Western Working Class Radicalism, 1890–1905," *Labor History* 7 (1966), 131–54.

11. In recent years the new western historians have sought to avoid use of the term *frontier*, believing it an ethnocentric label too often used to glorify expansion of a Euro-American East at the expense of Native Americans who already inhabited the "empty" West or of Hispanic settlers from Mexico who had also established a presence there. I seek to use the term here in a neutral sense to label a place of abrupt intersection between the pre-industrial West (and the Euro-American modes of thought and behavior popularly associated with it) with the urban and industrial West that followed. For a discussion of the new western history, see Patricia Nelson Limerick, Clyde A. Milner II, and Charles E. Rankin, eds., *Trails: Toward a New Western History* (Lawrence: University Press of Kansas, 1991).

12. Various aspects of the concept were initially developed in four articles by the author: "The Concept of the Wageworkers' Frontier: A Framework for Future Research," *Western Historical Quarterly* 18 (Jan. 1987), 39–55; "Patterns of Radicalism on the Wageworkers' Frontier," *Idaho Yesterdays* 30 (Fall 1986), 25–30; "Perceptions of Violence on the Wageworkers' Frontier: An American-Canadian Comparison," *Pacific Northwest Quarterly* 77 (1986), 52–57; "Illustrating the Wageworkers' Frontier: The New Northwest," *Montana, the Magazine of Western History* 38 (Autumn 1988), 38–49. The peculiarities of the wageworkers' frontier in Canada warrant a separate study. Basic sources for such a study are cited in bibliographies contained in A. Ross McCormack, *Reformers, Rebels, and Revolutionaries: The Western Canadian Radical Movement, 1899–1919* (Toronto: University of Toronto Press, 1977); Brian D. Palmer, *Working-Class Experience: The Rise and Reconstitution of Canadian Labour, 1800–1980* (Toronto: Butterworth & Co., 1983); David J. Bercuson, *Fools and Wise Men: The Rise and Fall of the One Big Union* (Toronto: McGraw-Hill Ryerson, 1978); Gregory S. Kealey and Peter Warrian, eds., *Essays in Canadian Working Class History* (Toronto: McClelland and Stewart, 1976); and Carlos A. Schwantes, *Radical Heritage: Labor, Socialism, and Reform in Washington and British Columbia, 1885–1917* (Seattle: University of Washington Press, 1979).

13. Vernon H. Jensen, *Heritage of Conflict: Labor Relations in the Nonferrous Metals Industry up to 1930* (Ithaca: Cornell University Press, 1950), 1–9; Mark Wyman, *Hard Rock Epic: Western Miners and the Industrial Revolution, 1860–1910* (Berkeley: University of California Press, 1979); Andrew Mason Prouty, *More Deadly Than War: Pacific Coast Logging, 1827–1981* (New York: Garland, 1985); Jerry Lembcke and William M. Tattam, *One Union in Wood: A Political History of the International Woodworkers of America* (New York: International Publishers, 1984). A similar situation prevailed on the southern Oregon coast and in northern California: see William G. Robbins, *Hard Times in Paradise: Coos Bay, Oregon* (Seattle: University of Washington Press, 1988); and Daniel A. Cornford, *Workers and Dissent in the Redwood Empire* (Philadelphia: Temple University Press, 1987). See also David Jay Bercuson, "Labour Radicalism and the Western Industrial Frontier," *Canadian Historical Review* 58 (1977), 154–75.

14. Richard H. Peterson, "The Frontier Thesis and Social Mobility on the Mining Frontier," *Pacific Historical Review* 44 (1975), 52–67. The rags-to-riches-to-rags legend of one famous mining entrepreneur is discussed in Duane A. Smith, *Horace Tabor: His Life and Legend* (Boulder: Colorado Associated University Press, 1973). See also John Fahey, *The Days of the Hercules* (Moscow: University Press of Idaho, 1978), and Richard H. Peterson, *Bonanza Rich: Lifestyles of the Western Mining Entrepreneurs* (Moscow: University of Idaho Press, 1991).

15. Richard Maxwell Brown, "The New Regionalism in America, 1970–1981," *Regionalism and the Pacific Northwest*, ed. William G. Robbins, Robert J. Frank, and Richard E. Ross (Corvallis: Oregon State University Press, 1983), 71–75. For a study of the contradictory nature of frontier images and

labor, see Howard Lamar, "From Bondage to Contract: Ethnic Labor in the American West, 1600–1890," in *The Countryside in the Age of Capitalist Transformation: Essays in the Social History of Rural America*, ed. Steven Hahn and Jonathan Prude (Chapel Hill: University of North Carolina Press, 1985), 293–324. In a sense I am seeking in this discussion of the wageworkers' frontier to update and elaborate upon an observation made more than 50 years ago by Selig Perlman and Philip Taft, who wrote of disputes in Rocky Mountain mining camps that "the extremes of violence in these labor struggles proceeded from no theory of revolution but from the general characteristics of the frontier." In John R. Commons, et al., *History of Labour in the United States, 1896–1932*, (4 vols. (1918–35; rpt. New York: Augustus M. Kelley, 1966), IV, 169.

16. Charles A. Siringo, *A Cowboy Detective: A True Story of Twenty-two Years with a World-Famous Detective Agency* (1912; rpt. Lincoln: University of Nebraska Press, 1989); Ben E. Pingenot, *Siringo* (College Station: Texas A&M University Press, 1989); Frank Morn, *"The Eye That Never Sleeps": A History of the Pinkerton National Detective Agency* (Bloomington: Indiana University Press, 1982), 160–63; Tacoma *Daily News*, April 5, 1894, pp.1, 2; Seattle *Press-Times*, May 20, 1891, p.1; Robert A. Campbell, "Blacks and the Coal Mines of Western Washington, 1888–1896," *Pacific Northwest Quarterly* 73 (1982), 146–55.

17. Lawrence H. Larsen, *The Urban West at the End of the Frontier* (Lawrence: Regents Press of Kansas, 1978); Walter Nugent, *Structures of American Social History* (Bloomington: Indiana University Press, 1981), 98–100; Rodman Wilson Paul, *Mining Frontiers of the Far West, 1848–1880* (New York: Holt, Rinehart and Winston, 1963); Henry Nash Smith, *Virgin Land: The American West as Symbol and Myth* (Cambridge, Mass.: Harvard University Press, 1950). A convenient source of regional economic statistics is Harvey S. Perloff, Edgar S. Dunn, Jr., Eric E. Lampard, and Richard F. Muth, *Regions, Resources, and Economic Growth* (Baltimore: Johns Hopkins Press, 1960). Some might argue that the Great Lakes timber and mineral country and the oil fields of the Southwest that opened in the early 20th century also belong to the wageworkers' frontier. It seems that the North country had a mystique all its own, distinct from that of the classic West with its promise of abundant, easily acquired arable land. As for the oil country, C. B. Glasscock writes in his 1938 classic, "The newly opening Oklahoma oil fields were closer to civilization, both in time and space, than were the great mining developments of the preceding half century. Modernized small cities such as Tulsa and Oklahoma City were only a few hours away. Great commercial and industrial centers such as Kansas City, St. Louis and Chicago could put men upon any piece of land within the entire state of Oklahoma as quickly as a Tulsa resident could have reached Muskogee a few years earlier." C. B. Glasscock, *Then Came Oil: The Story of the Last Frontier* (1938; rpt. Westport, Conn.: Hyperion Press, 1976, 227. Also see Roger M. Olien and Diana Davids Olien, *Oil Booms: Social Change in Five Texas Towns* (Lincoln: University of Nebraska Press, 1982).

18. David M. Emmons, *The Butte Irish: Class and Ethnicity in an American Mining Town, 1875–1925* (Urbana: University of Illinois Press, 1989), 62–63, 72.

19. Ray Allen Billington, *America's Frontier Heritage* (New York: Holt, Rinehart and Winston, 1966), 97–116 *passim*; Thomas C. Cochran, *Frontiers of Change: Early Industrialism in America* (New York: Oxford University Press, 1981), 50–77 *passim*; Earl Pomeroy, *The Pacific Slope: A History of California, Oregon, Washington, Idaho, Utah, and Nevada* (New York: Knopf, 1965); Emmons, *The Butte Irish*, 63.

20. "The Italian as a Track Laborer," *Railway Age Gazette* 53 (Aug. 16, 1912), 303. Among the studies of casual labor in the West are Carleton H. Parker, *The Casual Laborer and Other Essays* (New York: Harcourt, Brace and Howe, 1920); Roger A. Bruns, *Knights of the Road: A Hobo History* (New York: Methuen, 1980); Carlos A. Schwantes, *Coxey's Army: An American Odyssey* (Lincoln: University of Nebraska Press, 1985); and Eric H. Monkkonen, ed., *Walking to Work: Tramps in America, 1790–1935* (Lincoln: University of Nebraska Press, 1984). See also Donald Avery, *"Dangerous Foreigners": European Immigrant Workers and Labour Radicalism in Canada, 1896–1931* (Toronto: McClelland and Stewart, 1979), 16–64 *passim*.

21. Stephan Thernstrom and Peter Knights, "Men in Motion: Some Data and Speculations on Urban Population Mobility in 19th Century America," *Journal of Interdisciplinary History* 1 (Autumn 1970), 7–35; Carlos A. Schwantes, ed., *Bisbee: Urban Outpost on the Frontier* (Tucson: University of Arizona Press, 1992).

22. One observer estimated in 1914 that of the approximately 9,000 industrial wage earners in Butte, Montana, about one-quarter of them changed jobs annually. *Report of the Commission on Industrial Relations,* (64th Cong, 1st Sess., 1916, Senate Document 415, vol.4, p.3700.

23. Little has been published on operatives in the New Northwest. An exception for the sawmill workers is Norman H. Clark, *Mill Town: A Social History of Everett, Washington, from Its Earliest Beginnings on the Shores of Puget Sound to the Tragic and Infamous Event Known as the Everett Massacre* (Seattle: University of Washington Press, 1970), 91–93. Offering a useful comparison for California is Vicki L. Ruiz, *Cannery Women / Cannery Lives: Mexican Women, Unionization, and the California Food Processing Industry, 1930–1950* (Albuquerque: University of New Mexico Press, 1987).

24. The distinctions between craftsmen, operatives, and common laborers are examined in David Montgomery, *The Fall of the House of Labor* (Cambridge: Cambridge University Press, 1987). These three categories should not be interpreted as representing a labor hierarchy that ranged from the least to the most skilled, although laborers and operatives generally did not possess the technical know-how of the craftsmen, many of whom in pre–Civil War days had been trained in lengthy programs of apprenticeship. See W. J. Rorabaugh, *The Craft Apprentice: From Franklin to the Machine Age in America* (New York: Oxford University Press, 1986), esp.198–209.

25. Daniel Boorstin provides a useful discussion of America's geographical, political, technological, and cultural verges in his *Hidden History: Exploring Our Secret Past* (New York: Harper & Row, 1987), ix-xxv.

Chapter 2

1. Ira B. Cross, *A History of the Labor Movement in California* (Berkeley: University of California Press, 1935), 10–18; Rodman Wilson Paul, *Mining Frontiers of the Far West, 1848–1880* (New York, 1963), 37–55 *passim;* Duane A. Smith, *Rocky Mountain Mining Camps: The Urban Frontier* (Bloomington: Indiana University Press, 1967). See also David F. Selvin, *A Place in the Sun: A History of California Labor* (San Francisco: Boyd & Fraser, 1981); and Michael Kazin, *Barons of Labor: The San Francisco Building Trades and Union Power in the Progressive Era* (Urbana: University of Illinois Press, 1987).

2. *Overland Monthly* 19 (January 1892), 45; Cross, *Labor Movement in California,* 25–28; Roger W. Lotchin, *San Francisco, 1846–1856: From Hamlet to City* (New York: Oxford University Press, 1974), 84–87; Fred A. Shannon, *The Farmer's Last Frontier: Agriculture, 1860–1897* (New York: Farrar & Rinehart, 1945), 367.

3. John R. Stilgoe, *Metropolitan Corridor: Railroads and the American Scene* (New Haven: Yale University Press, 1983); Carleton H. Parker, *The Casual Laborer and Other Essays* (New York: Harcourt, Brace and Howe, 1920); Michael Malone, *The Battle for Butte: Mining and Politics on the Northern Frontier, 1864–1906* (Seattle: University of Washington Press, 1981); Murray Morgan, *Skid Road: An Informal Portrait of Seattle* (New York: Viking Press, 1951); Thomas J. Noel, *The City and the Saloon: Denver, 1858–1916* (Lincoln: University of Nebraska Press, 1982); R. D. McKenzie, "The Ecological Approach to the Study of the Human Community," in *The City,* [ed.] Robert E. Park, Ernest W. Burgess, and Roderick D. McKenzie (1929; rpt. Chicago: University of Chicago Press, 1967, 78–79.

4. Parker, *The Casual Laborer,* 79; Roger Bruns, *Knights of the Road: A Hobo History* (New York: Methuen, 1980), 136–37; foreman, Butler Contracting Co., to Governor Ernest Lister, Olympia, Wash., June 16, 1917, in Great Northern Papers (21.F.13.5B), Minnesota Historical Society, St. Paul.

5. William O. Douglas, *Go East, Young Man: The Early Years; The Autobiography of William O. Douglas* (New York: Random House, 1974), 76–78; John C. Schneider, "Tramping Workers, 1890–1920: A Subcultural View," in *Walking to Work: Tramps in America, 1790–1935,* ed. Eric H. Monkkonen (Lincoln: University of Nebraska Press, 1984), 218; Parker, *The Casual Laborer,* 61–89 *passim;* Robert L. Tyler, *Rebels of the Woods: The I.W.W. in the Pacific Northwest* (Eugene: University of Oregon Press, 1967); Charlotte Todes, *Labor and Lumber* (New York: International Publishers, 1931); Norman H. Clark, *Mill Town: A Social History of Everett, Washington, from Its Earliest Beginnings on the Shores of Puget Sound to the Tragic and Infamous Event Known as the Everett Massacre* (Seattle: University of Washington Press, 1970), 47–48, 80–82; Carlos A. Schwantes, "Leftward Tilt on the Pacific Slope: Indigenous Unionism and the Struggle against AFL Hegemony in the State of Washington," *Pacific Northwest Quarterly* 70

(1979), 24–34; David Jay Bercuson, "The One Big Union in Washington," *Pacific Northwest Quarterly* 69 (1978), 127–34. William Z. Foster, *Pages from a Worker's Life* (New York: International Publishers, 1939), 107–9. A similar situation existed in western Canada: see Donald Avery, *"Dangerous Foreigners": European Immigrant Workers and Labour Radicalism in Canada, 1896–1932* (Toronto: McClelland and Stewart, 1979), 16–64 passim.

6. Ernest Ingersoll, "From the Fraser to the Columbia," *Harper's New Monthly Magazine* 68 (1884), 871. It must be emphasized here that this kind of itinerancy was by no means limited to the West or to common laborers. It was a fact of work life throughout the United States, though less so in the slave South, and occasionally involved even skilled workers. In the New Northwest, itinerancy loomed large in proportion to the rest of the regional work force and significantly influenced labor history. On itinerant labor see Carey McWilliams, *Ill Fares the Land: Migrants and Migratory Labor in the United States* (Boston: Little, Brown, 1942); Jules Tygiel, "Tramping Artisans: The Case of Carpenters in Industrial America," *Labor History* 22 (1981), 348–76; Andrea Graziosi, "Common Laborers, Unskilled Workers: 1880–1915," *Labor History* 22 (1981), 512–44.

7. Alexander Campbell McGregor, *Counting Sheep: From Open Range to Agribusiness on the Columbia Plateau* (Seattle: University of Washington Press, 1982), 184–91; Schneider, "Tramping Workers," 218; *Industrial Union Bulletin*, Nov. 9, 1907, p.1. Mark Wyman notes the case of 32-year-old John Quinn, who, when he ran for sheriff of Butte in 1902, had already worked in mines in Arizona, Utah, and Idaho as well as Montana: *Hard Rock Epic: Western Miners and the Industrial Revolution, 1860–1910* (Berkeley: University of California Press, 1979), 59. Also see Ronald C. Brown, *Hard-Rock Miners: The Intermountain West, 1860–1920* (College Station: Texas A&M University Press, 1979), 3–19. A case study of itinerant workers in the hard-rock mining industry is Jim Foster, "The Ten Day Tramps," *Labor History* 23 (1982), 608–21.

8. Bruce Nelson, *Workers on the Waterfront: Seamen, Longshoremen, and Unionism in the 1930s* (Urbana: University of Illinois Press, 1988), 62–64.

9. Schneider, "Tramping Workers," 224; Clark C. Spence, "Knights of the Tie and Rail – Tramps and Hoboes in the West," *Western Historical Quarterly* 2 (1971), 5–19. For a discussion of "riding the rods," see Richard W. Etulain, *Jack London on the Road: The Tramp Diary and Other Hobo Writings* (Logan: Utah State University Press, 1979), 89–95; also Foster, *Pages from a Worker's Life*, 115–20.

10. E. Keough, "Characteristics of the Hobo," *Railway Age Gazette* 52 (June 21, 1912), 1566.

11. Of a total of 17,466 people employed in the lumber industry of Oregon and Washington in 1900, only 350 were not Caucasian. Classified as "colored" were Chinese, Japanese, African Americans, and Native Americans. See United States Immigration Commission, *Report*, 61st Cong., 2d Sess., 1911, SD 633, vol.25, "Immigrants in Industries," 344. Bureau of the Census, *Twelfth Census of the United States, Taken in the Year 1900, Population*, vol.1, pt.1, pp.609ff; Melvyn Dubofsky, *We Shall Be All: A History of the Industrial Workers of the World* (Chicago: 1969), 25–27; Philip S. Notarianni, Jr., and Joseph Stipanovich, "Immigrants, Industry, and Labor Unions: The American West, 1890–1916," *Journal of Historical Studies* 3 (Fall / Winter 1978), 1–14.

12. Quoted in Schneider, "Tramping Workers," 215. On race and ethnicity of railroad workers of the New Northwest, see W. Thomas White, "A History of Railroad Workers in the Pacific Northwest, 1883–1934," Ph. D. dissertation (University of Washington, 1981); Carlos A. Schwantes, "Protest in a Promised Land: Unemployment, Disinheritance, and the Origin of Labor Militancy in the Pacific Northwest, 1885–1886," *Western Historical Quarterly* 13 (1982), 373–90.

13. Paula Petrik, *No Step Backward: Women and Family on the Rocky Mountain Mining Frontier, Helena, Montana, 1865–1900* (Helena: Montana Historical Society Press, 1987); Marion S. Goldman, *Gold Diggers and Silver Miners: Prostitution and Social Life on the Comstock Lode* (Ann Arbor: University of Michigan Press, 1983); Ruth B. Moynihan, Susan Armitage, and Christiane Fischer Dichamp, eds., *So Much to Be Done: Women Settlers on the Mining and Ranching Frontier* (Lincoln: University of Nebraska Press, 1990).

14. Stewart Holbrook, *Holy Old Mackinaw: A Natural History of the American Lumberjack* (1956; rpt. New York: Ballantine Books, 1971).

15. There are numerous short descriptions of these districts but no analytical study of their role in western labor. See Harvey O'Connor, *Revolution in Seattle* (1964; rpt. Seattle: Left Bank Books, 1981), 64–65; Lowell S. Hawley and Ralph Bushnell Potts, *Counsel for the Damned: A Biography of George*

Francis Vanderveer (Philadelphia: Lippincott, 1953), 14–15, 43–52; and Morgan, *Skid Road*, 128, 188.

16. U.S. Bureau of the Census, *Bulletin 14: Proportion of the Sexes in the United States* (1904), 20. Murray Morgan describes Seattle's red light district in *Skid Road* 116–58 *passim*; on Butte see Joseph Kinsey Howard, *Montana: High, Wide, and Handsome* (1943; rpt. Lincoln: University of Nebraska Press, 1983), 93–97; David M. Emmons, *The Butte Irish: Class and Ethnicity in an American Mining Town, 1875–1925* (Urbana: University of Illinois Press, 1989), 22; and Malone, *The Battle for Butte*, 74–75.

17. "Erickson's: A Logger's Reverie," *Four L Bulletin* 7 (February 1925), 16, 44–46.

18. Daniel Rodgers, *The Work Ethic in Industrial America, 1850–1920* (Chicago: University of Chicago Press, 1978), 30–64 *passim*; Irwin Yellowitz, *Industrialization and the American Labor Movement, 1850–1900* (Port Washington, N.Y.: Kennikat Press, 1977), 37–46; E. V. Smalley, "Discontent of the Laboring Classes," *Northwest Magazine* 4 (February 1886), 25; Norman J. Ware, *The Labor Movement in the United States, 1860–1895: A Study in Democracy* (New York: D. Appleton & Co., 1929), 74; Gerald N. Grob, *Workers and Utopia: A Study of Ideological Conflict in the American Labor Movement, 1865–1900* (Chicago: Quadrangle, 1969), 44–47, 51; Lewis Perry, *Radical Abolitionism: Anarchy and the Government of God in Antislavery Thought* (Ithaca: Cornell University Press, 1973), 288–89, 302; David Montgomery, *Beyond Equality: Labor and the Radical Republicans, 1862–1872* (New York: Alfred A. Knopf, 1967), 25–44 *passim*; John Swinton, *A Momentous Question: The Respective Attitudes of Labor and Capital* (Philadelphia: Keller Publishing Co., 1895), 53–55; Ray Allen Billington, *Frederick Jackson Turner: Historian, Scholar, Teacher* (New York: Oxford University Press, 1973), 108–9, 198. See also Barry Herbert Goldberg, "Beyond Free Labor: Labor, Socialism, and the Idea of Wage Slavery, 1890–1920," Ph.D. dissertation (Columbia University, 1979).

19. The poem is quoted in Harold C. Livesay, *Samuel Gompers and Organized Labor in America* (Boston: Little, Brown, and Co., 1978), 14.

20. See David M. Emmons, *Garden in the Grasslands: Boomer Literature of the Central Great Plains* (Lincoln: University of Nebraska Press, 1971); and Norman Best, *A Celebration of Work*, ed. William G. Robbins (Lincoln: University of Nebraska Press, 1990), 9–33.

21. *Wealth and Resources of Oregon and Washington, the Pacific Northwest* (Portland: Union Pacific Railway, 1889), 1.

22. *West Shore* 10 (May 1884), 160. This episode lends credence to the argument of an indirect safety valve: Norman J. Simler, "The Safety-Valve Doctrine Re-evaluated," *Agricultural History* 32 (1958), 250–57; Carlos A. Schwantes, "Blessed are the Mythmakers? Free Land, Unemployment, and Uncle Sam in the American West," *Idaho Yesterdays* 27 (Fall 1983), 2–12; Ray Allen Billington, *Land of Savagery / Land of Promise: The European Image of the American Frontier in the Nineteenth Century* (New York: Norton, 1981).

23. Salem *Oregon Statesman*, Jan. 14, 1887; Oregon State Board of Immigration, *Oregon as It Is* (Salem, 1885); Oregon State Board of Immigration, *The Pacific Northwest: Its Wealth and Resources* (Portland [1891]), 4; *Wealth and Resources of Oregon and Washington*; Emmons, *The Butte Irish*, 257.

24. *West Shore* 3 (March 1878), 109.

25. Donald L. McMurry, *Coxey's Army: A Study of the Industrial Army Movement of 1894* (Boston, 1929), 183; *Solidarity*, Nov. 1, 1913, p.2; Portland *Oregonian*, April 17, 1886, p.2; Carlos A. Schwantes, *Coxey's Army: An American Odyssey* (Lincoln: University of Nebraska Press, 1985); Schwantes, "Blessed are the Mythmakers?" 2–12; Avery, "*Dangerous Foreigners*," 25–27; Richard White, "Poor Men on Poor Lands: The Back-to-the Land Movement of the Early Twentieth Century – A Case Study," *Pacific Historical Review* 49 (1980), 105–31 *passim*; Norman Clark, *Washington: A Bicentennial History* (New York: Norton, 1976), 138–39.

26. Frederick Jackson Turner, *The Frontier in American History* (1920; rpt. Huntington, N.Y.: Robert E. Krieger, 1976, 259–60. An excellent summary of recent critiques of Turner's approach to western history is Patricia Nelson Limerick, Clyde A. Milner II, and Charles E. Rankin, eds., *Trails: Toward a New Western History* (Lawrence: University Press of Kansas, 1991).

27. Fred A. Shannon, "A Post Mortem for the Labor-Safety-Valve Theory," *Agricultural History* 19 (1945), 36; Ellen von Nardroff, "The American Frontier as Safety Valve – The Life, Death, Reincarnation, and Justification of a Theory," *Agricultural History* 36 (1962), 123–42; Carter Goodrich and Sol Davison, "The Wage-Earner in the Westward Movement," pts. 1 and 2; *Political Science Quarterly* 50 (1935), 161–85, and 51

(1936), 61–116. The purpose of the latter two essays is to disprove the notion that a substantial number of eastern wageworkers moved to western lands. The authors say little about the origin of western wage earners and provide only skimpy data about the wage-earning easterners who moved west to take industrial jobs.

28. Seattle *Daily Press,* May 26, 1886, p.2.

29. *Industrial Union Bulletin* (Chicago), Feb. 27, 1909, p.2.

30. Melvyn Dubofsky, "Origins of Western Working Class Radicalism, 1890–1905," *Labor History* 7 (1966), 148. Workers at a rally in Spokane in 1890 had earlier voiced similar sentiments when they vowed to oppose employers' efforts to reduce them to the servile status they perceived to be the lot of eastern labor. Mrs. S. R. Keenan, the first woman ever to address a labor meeting in Spokane, informed her listeners that eastern workers, especially women, commonly believed that westerners had "no cause to organize and create a disturbance; that they should visit the East if they wished to see what downtrodden labor was." To this arguement Keenan responded, "If the Eastern people want to come out here, they must come up to our standards and not expect the people out here to drop down to theirs." Spokane *Daily Chronicle,* March 3, 1890, p.4. See also Carlos A. Schwantes, "Spokane and the Wageworkers' Frontier: A Labor History to World War I," in *Spokane and the Inland Empire: An Interior Pacific Northwest Anthology,* ed. David H. Stratton (Pullman: Washington State University Press, 1991), 122–41.

Chapter 3

1. See Carlos A. Schwantes, *Radical Heritage: Labor, Socialism, and Reform in Washington and British Columbia, 1885–1917* (Seattle: University of Washington Press, 1979).

2. Alexander P. Saxton, *The Indispensable Enemy: Labor and the Anti-Chinese Movement in California* (Berkeley: University of California Press, 1971), 113–37 *passim;* Carlos A. Schwantes, "Protest in a Promised Land: Unemployment, Disinheritance, and the Origin of Labor Militancy in the Pacific Northwest, 1885–1886," *Western Historical Quarterly* 13 (1982), 373–90.

3. James A. Halseth and Bruce A. Glasrud, "Anti-Chinese Movements in Washington, 1885–1886: A Reconsideration," in *The Northwest Mosaic: Minority Conflicts in Pacific Northwest History,* ed. James A. Halseth and Bruce A. Glasrud (Boulder: Pruett,

1977), 116–39; Jules A. Karlin, "The Anti-Chinese Outbreaks in Seattle, 1885, 1886," *Pacific Northwest Quarterly* 39 (1948), 103–30; Jules A. Karlin, "The Anti-Chinese Outbreak in Tacoma, 1885," *Pacific Historical Review* 27 (1954), 271–83.

4. Schwantes, "Protest in a Promised Land," 373–90; Ernest Ingersoll, "From the Fraser to the Columbia," *Harper's New Monthly Magazine* 68 (1884), 871; Saxton, *The Indispensable Enemy,* 271–73; Robert Edward Wynne, *Reaction to the Chinese in the Pacific Northwest and British Columbia, 1850–1910* (New York City: Arno, 1978).

5. Charles Pierce LeWarne, *Utopias on Puget Sound, 1885–1915* (Seattle: University of Washington Press, 1975).

6. Schwantes, "Protest in a Promised Land," 387–90.

7. On the secession of West Coast longshoremen, see Charles P. Larrowe, *Harry Bridges: The Rise and Fall of Radical Labor in the United States* 2d ed., rev. (Westport, Conn.: Lawrence Hill, 1972); and Bruce Nelson, *Workers on the Waterfront: Seamen, Longshoremen, and Unionism in the 1930s* (Urbana: University of Illinois Press, 1988). On secession in the paperworkers' union, see Robert H. Zieger, *Rebuilding the Pulp and Paper Workers' Union, 1933–1941* (Knoxville: University of Tennessee Press, 1984).

8. Carlos A. Schwantes, "Leftward Tilt on the Pacific Slope: Indigenous Unionism and the Struggle against AFL Hegemony in the State of Washington," *Pacific Northwest Quarterly* 70 (1979), 24–34.

9. Melvyn Dubofsky, *We Shall Be All: A History of the Industrial Workers of the World* (Chicago: Quadrangle, 1969).

10. Len De Caux, *The Living Spirit of the Wobblies* (New York: International Publishers, 1978), 57–68 *passim;* Robert L. Tyler, *Rebels of the Woods: The I.W.W. in the Pacific Northwest* (Eugene: University of Oregon Books, 1967).

11. Glen J. Broyles, "The Spokane Free Speech Fight, 1909–1910: A Study in IWW Tactics," *Labor History* 19 (1978), 238–52; Lowell S. Hawley and Ralph Bushnell Potts, *Counsel for the Damned: A Biography of George Francis Vanderveer* (Philadelphia: Lippincott, 1953), 176.

12. Harold M. Hyman, *Soldiers and Spruce: Origins of the Loyal Legion of Loggers and Lumbermen* (Los Angeles: Institute of Industrial Relations, University of California, Los Angeles, 1963); Robert L. Tyler, "The United States Government as Union Orga-

nizer: The Loyal Legion of Loggers and Lumbermen," *Mississippi Valley Historical Review* 47 (1960), 434–51.

13. Dubofsky, *We Shall Be All,* 447.

14. Alexander Campbell McGregor, *Counting Sheep: From Open Range to Agribusiness on the Columbia Plateau* (Seattle: University of Washington Press, 1982), 270.

15. John Fahey, *The Ballyhoo Bonanza: Charles Sweeny and the Idaho Mines* (Seattle: University of Washington Press, 1971), 112–15; Warren James Belasco, *Americans on the Road: From Autocamp to Motel, 1910–1945* (Cambridge, Mass.: M. I. T. Press, 1979), 105–16; Reynold Wik, *Henry Ford and Grass-Roots America* (Ann Arbor: University of Michigan Press, 1973); Alex McGregor, "From Sheep Range to Agribusiness: A Case History of Agricultural Transformation on the Columbia Plateau," *Agricultural History* 54 (1980), 11–27 *passim;* James H. Shideler, *Farm Crisis, 1919–1923* (Berkeley: University of California Press, 1957), 8, 80.

16. Carey McWilliams, *Ill Fares the Land: Migrants and Migratory Labor in the United States* (Boston: Little, Brown, 1942), 51–70 *passim;* Richard L. Neuberger, *Our Promised Land* (New York: Macmillan, 1938), 34–60 *passim.*

17. Michael P. Malone, *C. Ben Ross and the New Deal in Idaho* (Seattle: University of Washington Press, 1970), 31–50 *passim;* Neuberger, *Our Promised Land,* 61–84 *passim.*

18. Neuberger, *Our Promised Land,* 238–71 *passim;* Jonathan Dembo, *Unions and Politics in Washington State, 1885–1935* (New York: Garland Publishing, 1983), 590–615 *passim;* Richard C. Berner, *Seattle, 1921–1940: From Boom to Bust* (Seattle: Charles Press, 1992). Berner's study contains numerous chapters on Seattle labor in the 1920s and 1930s.

19. Carlos A. Schwantes, ed. *The Pacific Northwest in World War II* (Manhattan, Kans.: Sunflower University Press, 1986). This is a compilation of seven essays on the Second World War in the Pacific Northwest and Alaska.

20. Pete Daniel, Merry A. Foresta, Maren Stange, and Sally Stein, *Official Images: New Deal Photography* (Washington, D.C.: Smithsonian Institution Press, 1987).

59a. N. A. Forsyth photographed
miners at work nineteen hundred
feet below the streets of Butte circa
1910. Courtesy Montana Historical
Society.

Images of Empire: The Photographic Record

PART **2**

It is the most enterprising and unsettled Americans that come West; and when they have left their old haunts, broken their old ties, resigned the comforts and pleasures of their former homes, they are resolved to obtain the wealth and success for which they have come. They throw themselves into work with a feverish yet sustained intensity. They rise early, they work all day, they have few pleasures, few opportunities for relaxation. I remember in the young city of Seattle on Puget Sound to have found business in full swing at seven o'clock A.M.; the shops open, the streets full of people. Everything is speculative, land (or as it is usually called, "real estate") most so, the value of lots of ground rising or falling perhaps two or three hundred per cent in the year. No one has any fixed occupation; he is a storekeeper to-day, a ranch-man tomorrow, a miner next week. – James Bryce, *The American Commonwealth* (1911)

59. The Denny Regrade in Seattle symbolized the challenge of building a New Northwest. "The census of 1900 gave the city a population of 80,671, nearly double the figure of 1890. In the same year the first horseless carriage, an electric runabout, with a top speed of 20 miles an hour, appeared on the streets. Seattle, confident of its future, now took steps to extend its business district, cramped by the surrounding hills. The method of sluicing employed in Alaskan mining to remove hills caught the imagination of engineers and real estate developers, and workmen began to wash away the Jackson Street and Dearborn Street hills and part of Denny Hill. The loosened earth was used to fill in 1,400 acres of tideflats, making it available for factory sites. The venture was so successful that within the next 30 years 41,500,000 cubic yards of dirt were shifted." – *Washington, A Guide to the Evergreen State* (Portland: Binfords & Mort, 1941), 219. Courtesy Washington State Historical Society.

Building a New Northwest

I saw Tacoma in 1887, and again in 1889 and 1890, and the growth of the city in this short time was such that in both cases I could hardly recognize the place. It seemed as if some fairy had visited the town and changed every black stump into a four-story brick building by touching it with her wand. The cause of this sudden "spurt" was the completion of the Cascade Division of the Northern Pacific Railroad, and the Stampede Tunnel, which opened up the vast coal-fields along this road, and made the Pacific Coast cities independent of Pennsylvania coal. – Henry T. Finck, *The Pacific Coast Scenic Tour* (1890)

But over and through all of this progress and accomplishment there shines the mysterious and romantic light of a rude era that was so recent as to have involved even the middle-aged men of to-day. It was of the type of that of '49 in California. It was an era of new mining camps, of swarming tides of men thirsty for nuggets, of pistol-bristling sheriffs, of vigilantes, road-agents, Indian fights, stagecoaches, and all the motley characters that gave Bret Harte his imagination. You may meet some of the men who helped to rid the State [Montana] of outlaws by the holding of what they gayly spoke of as "necktie parties," and the application of hemp. They are apt to lounge into the clubs on any night, and with them you may see the best Indian "sign-talker" who ever lived, or that quick-handed, "scientific" ex-constable who proudly asserts that in the worst days he arrested hundreds of desperadoes bare-handed, without pulling his gun more than once or twice in his whole constabulary career. – Julian Ralph, *Our Great West: A Study of the Present Conditions and Future Possibilities of the New Commonwealths and Capitals of the United States* (1893)

60. Left: Long before the Denny Regrade, placer miners of the West perfected the technique of using water to move mountains. This photograph is of hydraulic mining on Prichard Creek in Idaho's Coeur d'Alene district. The practice, now outlawed, shot a high-pressure stream of water at benches and riverbanks to wash the material into sluices to recover gold. The device used only gravity to build up water pressure. Courtesy Barnard-Stockbridge Collection no.8-x302, University of Idaho Library.

61. Right: Another machine in the garden: a floating salmon wheel in the Columbia Gorge. The device, photographed by Carleton E. Watkins in 1882, efficiently and relentlessly scooped fish from the river. Like hydraulic mining and many early sawmills, it relied on water for power; and like hydraulic mining it was eventually outlawed because of its destructive impact on the environment. The first fish wheel on the Columbia dated from 1879; twenty years later, 76 were in operation. The last one stopped turning in 1934. Courtesy Oregon Historical Society, no.21623.

Wheels of Fortune

"You'll see the salmon-wheels 'fore long," said a man who lived "way back on the Washoogle," and whose hat was spangled with trout flies. "Those Chinook salmon never rise to fly. The canneries take them by the wheel." At the next bend we sighted a wheel — an infernal arrangement of wire gauze compartments worked by the current and moved out from a barge in shore to scoop up the salmon as he races up the river. California swore long and fluently at the sight, and more fluently when he was told of the weight of a good night's catch — some thousands of pounds. Think of the black and bloody murder of it. But you out yonder insist on buying tinned salmon, and the canneries cannot live by letting down lines.
— Rudyard Kipling, and published in *American Notes* (1890; Boston: Brown and Co., 1899), 54

62. The steamboat *Bailey Gatzert* gingerly negotiates the white water of the Columbia River as it squeezes through the Cascade Range in 1901. The age of steam came to the far Northwest with the appearance of the first steamboats on the Columbia and Missouri rivers. East of the Continental Divide, steamboat connections be- tween Saint Louis and Fort Union, near the confluence of the Missouri and Yellowstone rivers, were estab- lished as early as 1832 with the voy- age of the side-wheeler *Yellow Stone*. Elsewhere in the New Northwest, the first steamboat was the *Beaver,* a diminutive paddle boat constructed in England for the Hudson's Bay Company and placed in service on the lower Columbia River in 1836. It eventually ranged up the coast as far north as Russian Alaska. The ap- plication of steam to the region's sawmills originated in Portland in 1850, where one mill used a circular blade to produce lumber. The ma- chinery in the region's first sawmill, at Fort Vancouver, consisted of two men, one standing atop the log and another in a pit under it, whipsaw- ing it with a crosscut saw. Even with the application of water and steam power, many early mill mech- anisms were of this primitive type. Courtesy Oregon Historical Soci- ety, no.Gi 107.

63. A photograph of the New Northwest's pioneer industrial center, Oregon City, shows woolen and paper mills, a brick factory, and a powerhouse. Sometimes referred to as the "Lowell of the Pacific Coast," the city as an industrial site dated from 1864, when a woolen mill was established at the falls of the Willamette River. Two years later, the first paper mill on the West Coast initiated development of what was for years the city's most important industry. As this photograph illustrates, the New Northwest was not entirely devoted to the production of raw materials. "Manufacturing in Oregon has made slow but steady progress. The lumber industry plays the role of a general stimulant through its demand for logging locomotives, donkey-engines, steel cables, blocks and timber-cutting tools much of which equipment is made in the state." From *Oregon, End of the Trail* (Portland: Binford & Mort, 1940), 62. Courtesy Oregon Historical Society, no.005567.

64. Steam came to the woods long after it was used in the region's sawmills. John Dolbeer, a Humboldt Bay logger, invented the steam donkey in 1881 to yard logs to a railroad siding or a waterway. The machines, which were essentially upright engines that powered a capstan or, later, a windlass, came in many different sizes and configurations and were an integral part of logging in the Pacific Northwest for several decades. Courtesy Historical Photograph Collections, Washington State University Libraries, Pratsch no. 336.

65. Westbound Union Pacific freight at McCammon, Idaho, in 1892. No form of corporate enterprise did more to build the New Northwest than railroads during their heyday from the 1880s through the 1920s. Something so basic as the right-of-way represented the power of humans to triumph over nature, to transform a daunting landscape into standard measures of curvature and elevation and to shrink the vast distances of the New Northwest. Courtesy Idaho State Historical Society, no. 3332-B.

Steam Comes to the Woods

The mode of logging here is somewhat different than that of the Eastern, Southeastern and Central states. While the lumbering industry of all states has undergone great changes it is in the West that this has been the most marked. Within ten years, methods of logging have greatly changed; within twenty years they have been revolutionized. . . .

The early timberman was unable to operate by methods employed in the East. In the first place, timber was large and heavy, the country mountainous, so that it was impossible to use trucks as a means of hauling logs. Sleighs he was unable to use as the Pacific Slope has very little snow fall. So of necessity the pioneer logger always worked as near to water as possible, built his skid-roads and pulled his logs by means of ox-teams strung out one behind the other. . . . In this manner the logs were dragged to the water's edge, placed into booms, and floated to the saw mills. . . .

With the introduction of the donkey engine the oxen rapidly disappeared, not thrown on the scrap pile like antiquated machinery, but down the throats of the husky loggers. These engines, built especially for the purpose, handle logs by means of a steel cable operated from the drums of the engine; the engine being anchored at a landing it can haul the logs from a radius of 2,500 feet, or even more, to the loading platform where they are placed on cars and taken to the mills. — *Industrial Worker,* Nov. 23, 1911, p. 3

66. Railroad Avenue in Seattle about 1909. The city had earlier set aside a strip of land 120 feet wide to provide transcontinental railroads access to the heart of the community. Nationwide railroad connections gave daily life in Seattle and other parts of the New Northwest a new contour by opening distant markets to local products and thus stimulating industry and creating more jobs. Rail connections guaranteed neither metropolitan status nor future prosperity, but by the eve of World War I it was axiomatic that no place of consequence would exist beyond the sound of a locomotive whistle. Courtesy Special Collections Division, University of Washington Libraries, UW no. 1676.

67. Construction workers prepare to extend the tracks of the Chicago, Milwaukee & St. Paul Railway west across a coulee near Choteau, Montana, in 1915. Although this branch never extended any farther than Agawam, a few miles away, the optimism embodied in the impressive size of the bridge adds new meaning to the observation of James Bryce that westerners "seem to live in the future rather than the present; not that they fail to work while it is called to-day, but that they see the country not merely as it is, but as it will be, twenty, fifty, a hundred years hence, when the seedlings shall have grown to forest trees." Unfortunately for the management of the Chicago, Milwaukee and St. Paul, its vision of the future did not include the competition from automobiles and trucks that caused Milwaukee Road tracks across Montana to be abandoned well before a century had passed. James Bryce, *The American Commonwealth,* rev. ed. (New York: Macmillan, 1911), II, 899. Courtesy Milwaukee Road Collection, Milwaukee Public Library.

Gray's Harbor — Broadway looking south from Satsop Ave. August 19, 1889.

68. Aberdeen on Washington's Grays Harbor, looking south along Broadway in 1889. The New Northwest in the late nineteenth century was characterized by the juxtaposition of a rapidly developing urban-industrial complex with hauntingly beautiful virgin land. As late as 1890, some places, notably the Olympic Mountains across Puget Sound from Seattle and Tacoma, had yet to be entered by white explorers. Aberdeen's still tentative appearance recalls a quip made about another of the region's urban outposts. "Astoria, however, means to grow. It has already a large hotel, which the timber has crowded down against the tide-washed flats; a saw-mill which is sawing away for dear life, because if it stopped the forest would push it into the river, on whose brink it has courageously effected lodgement." Charles Nordhoff, "The Columbia River and Puget Sound," *Harper's New Monthly Magazine* 48 (1874), 338–48. Courtesy Special Collections Division, University of Washington Libraries, UW no.4373.

69. Instant community: Twin Falls, Idaho, in 1905 when it was less than a year old. The area, which eventually came to be known as the Magic Valley, seemed to underscore Bryce's observation that westerners "see all round about them railways being built, telegraph wires laid, steamboat lines across the Pacific projected, cities springing up in the solitudes, and settlers making the wilderness blossom like the rose. Their imagination revels in these sights and signs of progress, and they gild their own struggles for fortune with the belief that they are the missionaries of civilization and the instruments of Providence in the greatest work the world has seen." James Bryce, *The American Commonwealth,* rev. ed. (New York: Macmillan, 1911), II, 895–96. Courtesy Idaho State Historical Society, no.D 73–2.24.

Taming the Snake River near the Idaho-Wyoming Border in 1910

At eight o'clock the whistle of the steam shovel blew, the muckers began shoveling, the skinners started up their horses to drag the slips around, the hard-rock men, those who held drills sitting on gunnysacks to keep from freezing to the bed of the Snake, began their poetry of motion. Machines chugged and spluttered, pumps sloshed and gurgled, and the members of the surveying party set up the level or the transit – or at least, I did, since that was my job – and we drove stakes with tacks in them to indicate where the dirt and rock should be excavated, where and how high it should be piled on the dikes and waste banks, where the wooden forms for the concrete should be built. – Elliot Paul, *Desperate Scenery* (New York: Random House, 1954), 180

70. The human as machine: the camera of Russell Lee captured this enduring image of shearing sheep in Malheur County, Oregon, May 1941. The photograph evokes the sights and smells of a job that was done every spring in many areas of the Northwest: "At shearing time – late May and early June – the big sheds on sheep ranches are busy places. . . . Professional shearers travel in crews from ranch to ranch. Many start out early in the year and follow the season from Mexico to Montana.

"Shearing weather is usually hot, and the wool is oily and heavy. Wranglers shove, tug, and whoop as they drive five or six sheep at a time down the runway to each pen. . . . As the sheep enter the jug [pen], each shearer catches a ewe by a hindleg and hauls her to a sitting position. He begins shearing at the head, going down the throat or between the ears. . . . As the dirty gray fleece folds off, leaving the sheep a clean white or whitish yellow the shearer bunches the wool with his feet and hands, ties it with a string, drops it over the side of his jug, almost with a single motion. At the end of the day he knows how many sheep he has sheared and how much he has earned by the number of strings remaining in his belt. A shearer who can clip 200 sheep a day with the power shears, or 100 with the hand shears, is the object of considerable admiration to neighbors, buyers, idle herders, and other spectators.

"While the shearer straightens his back and smokes a cigarette, his helper sweeps the tags out of the pen. The tags – fragments of wool matted with dirt and manure – follow the fleeces into an 8-foot wool sack suspended from a 12-foot platform, and packed solidly – but not too solidly – by a 'stomper' who emerges from the sack as it fills. His is very hard work, for the wool, full of dirt and ticks, rolls in on him; his spot is the hottest and grimiest in the shed. . . . In the heat the odors of men and sheep blend into one master stench compounded of sweat, oily wool, sheep manure, and tobacco." – *Montana, A State Guide Book* (New York: Viking Press, 1939), 197–98. Courtesy Library of Congress, no. 11604 F3439095.

Human Machines

FOLIO **2**

Mr. Shannon. Those fellows that have got an easy place in the mine, where the air is good, and they always have a good word for the company for giving them the job. But they are not down where the actual work has got to be done, or where the heat is intense, where you don't eat anything and where you drink a keg of water and never urinate once in the 24 hours – you sweat it out. Them are the places, and you gentlemen ought to take a look at them.

Commissioner O'Connell. I think some of us were down last night in the mines; I was down.

Mr. Shannon. Now, these buzzy machines [pneumatic drills], they grind the dust up extra fine, and it comes out without the old method of clearing itself, and you inhale every bit of that dust as it comes out. The dust settles in your lungs and you can't get away from it. You are right there facing it, and it is pumped into you, the same as the hose turned on you. And the man down below you shoveling, he inhales it just as bad as you.
– Testimony of Joe Shannon, miner, before the U.S. Commission on Industrial Relations, Butte, Montana, August 1914

And so the logger, he finds that he is nothing but a living machine, not even treated so well as a horse. When the horse is out of work he is glad of it. When the wageworker is out of work he is up against it. They turn the hose on him in Sacramento. – Testimony of J. P. Thompson, Industrial Workers of the World organizer, before U.S. Commission on Industrial Relations, Seattle, Washington, August 1914

Coal mines are "inspected" about after this fashion: On the arrival at the mine of the inspector he is taken "in tow" by the boss, escorted to "the house," where he is dined and wined and made "comfortable." Then with the boss at his elbow, he is taken into the mine. This has been done when no miners are about, but it is well understood that it is as much as a miner's job is worth for him to suggest anything to the inspector, who usually goes away without talking to a miner unless in the presence of the boss.

"Inspection" under these circumstances is a farce. The miners could not tell the inspector if they dared to do so, of the true condition in the mine. There are mines in this state now, in which, unless changes are made, explosions are due before long. At least that is what miners tell me, and I believe them. But corporation attorneys and bamboozled coroner's juries would have us believe that this criminal neglect, which is practical[ly] murder, comes from "the providence of God." – John R. Rogers, Populist governor of Washington 1897–1901, Seattle *Call,* May 9, 1895

Rev. McGill. Now, up here at this Milwaukee Tunnel, where about a thousand men, I think, perhaps six hundred to a thousand men are employed during the ordinary season of the year, the timekeeper told me that they change the ordinary men – that the average stay of the men was five days, about five days. The day I was there there were 90 men quit. He showed me a bundle that he said contained 90 certificates.

Commissioner Lennon. Time Checks?

Rev. McGill. Time checks; yes, sir; for the men. They pay those men in two checks and they won't pay them until late in the afternoon, just before the train departs. They pay them in one check, the amount of their fare to Seattle; and if there is anything left to come to them, they give them another check. There were 90 men either discharged or quit that day, out of about 300 men at that end of the tunnel.

– Testimony of Oscar H. McGill, social services secretary, Methodist Church in Seattle, to the U.S. Commission on Industrial Relations, Seattle, Washington, August 1914

71. Boring a tunnel, probably on the Spokane, Portland & Seattle Railway, about 1908 to link Spokane and Portland via the Columbia River valley. The "North Bank Road" may well have been the finest piece of railway engineering in the entire region. Courtesy Eastern Washington State Historical Society, no.L86-255.

No Funeral

In 1907, when the S. P. & S. railroad was being built along the north bank of the Columbia River from Spokane to Portland, I worked for a railroad grading outfit near White Salmon, Washington. The job was a typical Western layout, and the rockmen, muckers and skinners came from all over the West. In the towns along the line the sky was the limit in "entertainment"; they were full of gamblers, prostitutes and every other species that preyed upon Western workers.

The "working stiffs," totally unorganized, had to accept pretty much whatever wages, hours and working and living conditions the bosses decided upon. How little a worker's life was valued was illustrated one day when two rockmen, caught by a premature blast, were blown to bits. All we found of them was a shoe with a torn-off foot inside. The hard-boiled boss hefted this in his hand a moment, and remarking, "Well, I guess we can't have a funeral over that," threw the grisly object into the swirling Columbia River. — William Z. Foster, *Pages from a Worker's Life* (New York: International Publishers, 1939), 36

Timber Beasts

Many of the timber beasts (loggers) are of Scandinavian stock. Some students of folklore say that the Scandinavians created the legendary Paul Bunyan by bringing to America their tales of Thor, the Norse god of indomitable strength. They are prodigious chewers of *snus* (Dan. and Sw. snuff), and tellers of tales; and they are proud of their prowess in a difficult and dangerous occupation. – *Montana, A State Guide Book* (New York: Viking Press, 1939), 308

72. Faller at the base of a Douglas fir in the 1920s. He has tossed his crosscut saw and ax to the ground. Some stands of Douglas fir on Washington's Olympic Peninsula were unbelievably thick: "Humptulips was the logging outlet for the famous '21–9' (township 21, range 9) stand of Douglas fir, the greatest in the Northwest. Towering timber stood so dense that trees had to be felled in the same direction for lack of space. In one of the Humptulips saloons of that time, a garrulous foreman boasted: 'Give me enough snoose and Swedes and I'll log 21–9 like it was a hayfield, dump the toothpicks into the south fork and ride 'em to tidewater like they was rocking horses.'" – *Washington, A Guide to the Evergreen State* (Portland: Binfords & Mort, 1941), 558. Courtesy Forest History Society.

73. A logger poses with a large tree typical of those that awed men who relocated to the New Northwest from the forests of the Great Lakes. Courtesy Historical Photograph Collections, Washington State University Libraries, Pratsch no.408.

74. A load of logs from Wrenshall, Minnesota, containing 2,150 board feet of lumber, was undoubtedly a source of pride in that state's timber country. It was photographed in March 1899, not long before the nation's timber frontier shifted to the New Northwest, where a single tree could yield that much lumber. Courtesy Minnesota Historical Society, no. 11465.

75. The 1941 log drive on Idaho's Clearwater River. Almost every spring from 1928 until 1971, a year's harvest of logs made the ninety-mile journey down the river to the mill at Lewiston. Most drives lasted two to three weeks, although some were finished in a week, and one required eighty days. This technique, used at various times on other rivers of the New Northwest, pitted life against logs and meant enduring cold water and raw winds. Men used pikes and peaveys and an occasional stick of dynamite to break up jams and herd errant logs off sandbars and back into the current. They needed strength and agility as they jumped from log to log to keep the mass moving. Courtesy Eastern Washington State Historical Society, no. L85–143.13.

Word Origins: From *Skid Road* to *Skidrow*

The word skidrow, *often used to denote a depressed area of town, is a corruption of the original* skid road, *derived from one of the early-day technologies for moving logs to tidewater on Puget Sound. In Seattle,* skid road *is still the preferred term.*

The swamper has the work of slashing or clearing away the timber for the penetration of skid roads. His duties are more deliberate than those of the rest, and scarcely as severe. He usually gets the start on the spring work, and in many instances works the year round. His wages are about $50 per month.

The skidder follows up the swamper, levels the road and puts in the skids, which are small round sticks of timber laid crossways of the road at intervals of eight feet for the logs to be hauled across. His work required exactness and skill in grading and he is paid, usually, about $60 per month.

But the one occupying the truly non-poetical position is the greaser. His paraphernalia complete consists of a swab, a bucket of grease and a pair of oil-soaked overalls. It is he who follows between the cattle and the log on a "turn," and, swab in hand, daubs each skid at regular intervals to prevent friction and save the oxen. When the greaser is just learning his trade he is often allowed to work along in front of the cattle until he gets so he can grease between the oxen and the log without danger of being jammed by the latter. . . . The greaser's wages are about $40 per month.
– Seattle *Press,* Jan. 23, 1891, p.8

76. A Clark Kinsey photograph of workers at the Brookings Lumber Company. Courtesy Special Collections Division, University of Washington Libraries, C. Kinsey no.277.

77. Spar tree: "The days of ox-team logging were over; and the introduction of the powerful donkey engine and the 'high-lead,' or spar tree, to which great logs were jerked with taut steel cables, had brought logging to a high level of efficiency. With vast profits to be made, work was speeded ahead with little heed to accident prevention, timber breakage, or destruction of young growth." – *Washington, A Guide to the Evergreen State* (Portland: Binfords & Mort, 1941), 168. Courtesy Oregon Historical Society, no.5131.

Loggers as Seen by Management

Mr. Thompson: What kind of men usually work in the logging camps and in and around the mills?
Mr. Page: In the logging camps; that is, in the logging camps proper that get out the logs, that is skilled labor, and it is composed largely of young men and mostly of unmarried men.

They are a high-strung class of fellows and reckless; they are in a reckless business, a risky business, and they throw their money away; they are men of that kind.
– Testimony of Paul E. Page, president of Page Lumber Company, Seattle, Washington, August 1914, *Report of the Commission on Industrial Relations,* 64th Cong., 1st Sess., 1916, Senate Document 415, vol.5, p.4250

Technology and the Logging Landscape

Sharp declivities, now denuded of spruce, cedar, and hemlock, indicate the site of former high-lead logging, which is characterized by the network of cables, blocks, and guy lines strung from spars (trees denuded of limbs), along which logs are pulled by donkey engines from one ridge to the other. High climbers – whose insurance rates indicate the great risks of their calling – trim and top 200 foot trees, up which they climb with the aid of spurs and a rope loop attached to a belt. Out in the timber a chokerman places a heavy wire slip-loop, or choker, around a log and a rigging-slinger attaches this loop to the main cable, when the hooker yells "Hi," then the whistle-punk presses an electric grip and the donkey 1,500 feet away, whistles a short, sharp blast. The donkey-puncher, or engine operator, "opens her up" and the log rises above stumps and brush as he yards it to the landing. As soon as the chaser has unhooked the log, a haulback returns the choker to the woods. – *Oregon, End of the Trail* (Portland: Binfords & Mort, 1940), 369

79. Interior of a sawmill in Port Ludlow, Washington. Puget Sound's first steam-powered mill dates from 1853; by the end of the 1860s the number had grown to more than forty. "At the mills, all is hurry and excitement. Coasting and foreign vessels are lying at the wharves, some discharging freight or ballast, while others are loading with the manufactured lumber, which varies from the heavy square timber a hundred and thirty feet in length down to laths which require a hundred to make up a bundle. The principal mills on Puget Sound are of an extensive scale. Of these, that at Port Madison is one of the best, sawing a hundred thousand feet of lumber daily; although the Port Gamble mill cuts a greater amount, employs more hands, and is by far the most extensive establishment of its kind in the Territory, being known under the name of 'Puget Mill Company.' Two hundred men are employed about the mill, and the same number in the logging camps." – Charles M. Scammon, "Lumbering in Washington Territory," *Overland Monthly* 5 (July 1870), 55–60. Courtesy Special Collections Division, University of Washington Libraries, UW no. 5056.

78. Few workers lived more dangerous lives than the high rigger employed in the logging industry. He looped his belt around the trunk of a spar tree, drove his spurs into the bark, and casually walked up its side to the top. At a point one hundred to two hundred feet above the ground, he "braced himself at a sickening angle against the swaying trunk, and, with a flow of cheerful profanity, severed with deft strokes of his razor-edged axe the green plume that rose above him; the shock of the falling crest sent the trunk and the logger on it gyrating dizzily through the air." – *Washington, A Guide to the Evergreen State* (Portland: Binfords & Mort, 1941), 168. Courtesy Oregon Historical Society, Drake no. 348.

Workers as Automatons

Saw mill work is monotonous and uninteresting. Like all machine tenders, the saw mill worker is reduced to a mere automaton. The pace is set by machinery speeded up to the limit of human endurance. The day's work consists of a continuous repetition of the same motions, at top speed. The work of saw mill employees is also exceedingly dangerous. Few men who have worked as sawyers for any length of time are possessed of a sound pair of hands, and many have lost one or more of their fingers. Often it is the whole hand. Most of the other jobs in a saw mill are equally dangerous. A single mis-step or a slip would mean death or mutilation in the whirling, unguarded machinery. – James Rowan, *The I. W. W. in the Lumber Industry* (Seattle: Lumber Workers Industrial Union no. 500 [192?]), 8

80. "Lumber alley" in the town of Potlatch, Idaho, where local boosters claimed title to the largest white pine sawmill in the world. "Winter or summer, workers contended with noise so loud it prohibited talk, especially inside the saw and planing mills," notes the historian Keith C. Petersen in *Company Town* (Pullman: Washington State University Press; and Moscow, Idaho: Latah County Historical Society, 1987), 78. "Crews became proficient at sign language." In this way they would tell stories, joke, and even swear. A Greek worker recalled that sign language enabled him to make friends before he could speak English. But, as Petersen warned, communication was not infallible: one worker chewed off another's ear in a fight that ensued when he misinterpreted a hand signal comment about his sister. Courtesy Idaho State Historical Society, no. 1158–53.

81. Shipping lumber in Washington. "The number of ships awaiting cargoes in the towns [on Puget Sound] is a matter of surprise to strangers, the contrast being so great between the small forest of masts and the few scattered houses discernible. Were it not for the heavy puffing of the steam the towns would seem to be arcadian hamlets. The mill companies own their own ships, so they have a double advantage. The lumber is shipped to all parts of the world, and the demand cannot be supplied." – *Puget Sound Business Directory* (Olympia, Wash., 1872). Courtesy Library of Congress, no. 11601 2–62 72997.

Skilled Labor?

Mr. Brown. The per cent of skilled men in sawmills is very small. In a sawmill employing 100 men the only skilled men would be the engineer, the filer, the head sawyer, the edger man, and perhaps a head plainer. That is about all the really skilled men that would be required around a sawmill. – Testimony of J. G. Brown, president of the International Union of Timber Workers, Seattle, Washington, August 1914, *Report of the United States Industrial Commission,* 64th Cong., 1st Sess., 1916, Senate Document 415, vol. 5 p. 4210

Lumber Production on Puget Sound

The lumber business is still the most important industry in Tacoma, and will probably long remain so. In 1873 there was one sawmill on the premises, and now there are seventeen, employing nearly fifteen hundred men, and with a combined capacity for turning out more than a million and a quarter feet a day. It is interesting to see these mills at work. There is one at which the steamers on the way to Olympia stop to take in water, so that passengers have time to watch the chain which, like a moving cable, carries down the debris of the timber in a flume-like trough, high in the air, and throws it down on a pile which is kept burning constantly. One cannot suppress the thought what a boon the fuel thus wasted would be to the poor in our Eastern cities. Vessels are always seen loading to carry the available part of the timber to all parts of the world. – Henry T. Finck, *The Pacific Coast Scenic Tour* (New York: C. Scribner's Sons, 1890), 220

82. Officers and crew of the *Parchim,* photographed in the sawmill town of Port Blakely, Washington, circa 1893. Stevedores needed at least ten days to lay down a cargo of lumber, one stick at a time, in the hold of the typical sailing vessel. A fleet of ships hauled lumber from the New Northwest to markets as distant as China and Australia. Courtesy San Francisco Maritime National Historical Park, no.F9.12,446n1.

83. Shipbuilders, probably in Astoria about 1910. Construction of wooden ships was an important industry on the lower Columbia River and Puget Sound until after World War I. Courtesy Oregon Historical Society, no.1262.

Climbing Jacob's Ladder

On my first day aboard the *Pegasus* the mate lined us all up and ordered those who had never been to sea before to stand aside. A few stepped out, but not I. I was determined to be a sailor from the start. The mate, however, was quite wise to me and shouted, "Hey you, go aloft and work with those men on the main skysail yard."

I felt a stab of fear; for the skysail was the highest of all, except on ships that carried sails called, suggestively enough, "angels' foot-stools." I took to the rigging as the mate watched me from the deck. Up I went past the main, lower-topsail, upper-topsail, top-gallant and royal yards, until I finally climbed the swaying "Jacob's Ladder" up to the dizzy skysail yard. At the "futtock" rigging, where for about eight feet one actually climbs upside down, I thought I was a goner. But I made it. The men on the skysail yard laughed and told me to just hang on while they did the work. After that I had no further trouble about climbing.

The sailor's work aloft was very dangerous. Often the ratlines upon which he stepped were rotten and gave way. On the yards he stood on a foot rope that was always slack and slippery and which frequently broke under his weight. He might also be thrown from the yards by the wild pitching of the ship, the motion aloft being much greater than on deck. Or he could be dragged off the yards by the wind while he was making sail fast during a storm. Perhaps as many were killed by falls as were washed overboard. Aboard one ship that I was on, an apprentice, on the previous voyage, had his back broken by a fall from aloft. In the rigging the sailor's motto was, "One hand for the ship and one hand for myself." – William Z. Foster, *Pages from a Worker's Life,* (New York: International Publishers, 1939), 67

84. Hauling in fish. According to the federal census of 1900, there were 5,944 fishermen and oystermen in Oregon and Washington. Almost one-third of them were Scandinavians. "No Asiatics are engaged in salmon fishing for the canneries. Their labor, unlike that employed on the Frazer River in British Columbia, where the Japanese have become an important element among the fishermen, is entirely [confined] within the canneries." – United States Immigration Commission, *Report,* 61st Cong., 2d Sess., 1911, SD 633, vol. 25, "Immigrants in Industries," 389. Courtesy Special Collections Division, University of Washington Libraries, A. Curtis no. 16021.

85. Workers shoveled mountains of snow to build the Great Northern Railway through the Cascade Range of Washington during the winter of 1892–93. A decade earlier, when the Northern Pacific extended its main line across northern Idaho and western Montana, work continued through the winter as one crew shoveled snow so that another could lay track. Courtesy Washington State Historical Society.

86. Ditch diggers in Port Angeles, Washington, formed part of the New Northwest's ubiquitous army of manual laborers. Courtesy Special Collections Division, University of Washington Libraries, A. Curtis no. 29682.

Manual Laborers: Muckers and Roustabouts

Throughout the winter [of 1910–11] for which we were so hastily preparing, we would need a force of at least 400 men, of whom 350 would work with their hands, manipulating tools, driving stoneboats, sleds or scrapers, drilling and blasting rock; mixing and placing concrete, doing rough carpentry on forms and camp buildings, rigging and operating heavy machinery; installing and maintaining electrical equipment; and most important of all, being just plain "muckers" and "roustabouts" with picks and shovels, strong backs and sturdy shoulders. – Elliott Paul, *Desperate Scenery* (New York: Random House, 1954), 84

MUCKING CONTEST
MINERS PICNIO
KELLOGG IDA
AUG. 16TH 1913

87. Play as work: a mucking contest at the Miners' Picnic in Kellogg, Idaho, on August 16, 1913. The backbreaking work of mucking or shoveling was often a step toward becoming a miner – in the narrowest sense, one who drilled, loaded, and detonated the holes. Strong drillers also competed against one another, often practicing for months for public contests. On the job a miner could work alone at single-jacking, turning a drill with one hand and wielding a three-pound hammer with the other. In double-jacking, used where space permitted, two men worked together, one swinging an eight-pound hammer and another turning the drill between blows. In the candle-lit darkness, a mistake might easily result in smashed fingers and broken limbs. Machine drills appeared as early as the 1870s, but hand drilling persisted into the twentieth century. Tramming, a third type of work underground, involved pushing the ore cars and required the least skill.

Hand drilling and blasting with black powder was slow, laborious, and dangerous. Although innovations like dynamite and the pneumatic drills made work easier, they posed serious health hazards. Early versions of pneumatic drills spewed out such thick clouds of silicosis-causing dust that they were aptly termed widow-makers. Courtesy Idaho State Historical Society, no.79–142.1.

88. Mining lead in Osburn, near Kellogg, Idaho, in 1912. "Below it the river bottoms look like a caricature of a graveyard, and above it the denuded mountains declare the potency of lead. . . . West of Kellogg with its miracles of machinery, there is still to be seen a poisoned and dead or dying landscape. Trees slain by the invisible giant still stand with lifeless limbs and with roots still sucking the poisoned earth. But gradually the blight thins, the flora look up to new strength, and the drive becomes increasingly lovely." – *Idaho, A Guide in Word and Picture* (Caldwell: Caxton Printers, 1937), 334. Courtesy Barnard-Stockbridge Collection, no.8-A282–4, University of Idaho Library.

89. Miners from Kellogg undergoing experimental electrolytic treatment for lead poisoning. Lead poisoning was only one of many perils facing underground miners. In some parts of the West, temperatures in mines two or three thousand feet below the surface rose to well over 100 degrees, and miners died of heat prostration. Courtesy Idaho State Historical Society, no.79.92.69.

Technology and Miners

When the power drills were introduced the work of the miners was changed. The men did not object to the installation of the machines, but many skillful miners were not physically capable of handling one of the big sluggers. No consideration was shown to them; they were put to running cars, shoveling ore, or as roustabouts at fifty cents a day less than the miners had been receiving. This would make a corresponding reduction in their standard of living. – William D. Haywood, *Bill Haywood's Book* (New York: International Publishers, 1929), 80

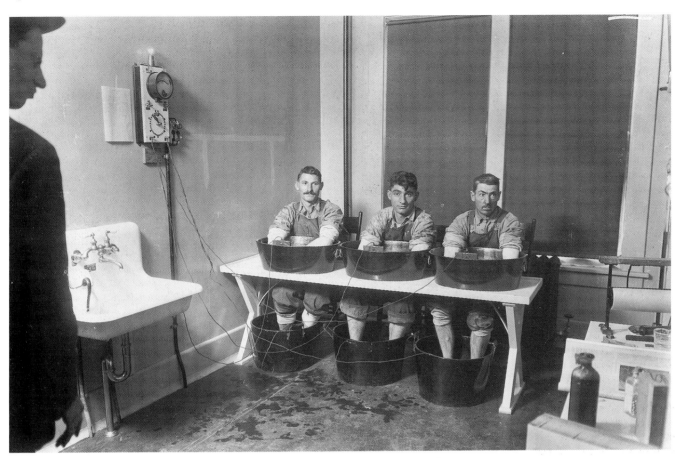

90. Salmon cannery, Astoria, Oregon. Thirty-eight canneries were located on the lower Columbia River in 1883, twenty-four of these in Astoria. Together they packed 630,000 cases that year. At the rate of one fish filling eighteen one-pound cans and four dozen cans making a case, it was estimated that the seventeen hundred boats on the river caught 1,680,000 salmon. Courtesy Oregon Historical Society, no.28194.

Chinese Labor

Mr. Lowman. Many years ago, when the salmon-canning industry was established, Chinese were practically the only labor available, and to-day they are the expert producers of canned salmon in the packing department. A Chinaman of 25 or 30 years experience knows all of those little things that you and I would have to devote as long an apprenticeship as he did in order to learn it, because his intelligence from that point of view is equal to ours, and I am not ashamed to say it. — Testimony of Will A. Lowman, president of Puget Sound Salmon Canneries Association, Seattle, Washington, August 1914, *Report of the Commission on Industrial Relations,* 64th Cong., 1st Sess., 1916, Senate Document 415, vol.5 p.4367

Kipling on Canning

The steamer halted at a rude wooden warehouse built on piles in a lonely reach of the [Columbia] river, and sent in the fish. I followed them up a scale-strewn, fishy incline that led to the cannery. The crazy building was quivering with the machinery on its floors, and a glittering bank of tin-scraps twenty feet high showed where the waste was thrown after the cans had been punched. Only Chinamen were employed on the work, and they looked like blood-besmeared yellow devils, as they crossed the rifts of sunlight that lay upon the floor. When our consignment arrived, the wooden boxes broke of themselves as they were dumped down under a jet of water, and the salmon burst out in a stream of quick-silver. A Chinaman jerked up a twenty-pounder, beheaded and detailed it with two swift strokes of a knife, flicked out its internal arrangements with a third, and cast it into a bloody dyed tank. The headless fish leaped from under his hands as though they were facing a rapid. Other Chinamen pulled them from the vat and thrust them under a thing like a chaffcutter, which, descending, hewed them into unseemly red gobbets fit for the can. More Chinamen with yellow, crooked fingers, jammed the stuff into the cans, which slid down some marvelous machine forthwith, soldering their own tops as they passed. Each can was hastily tested for flaws, and then sunk, with a hundred companions, into a vat of boiling water, there to be half cooked in a few minutes. The cans bulged slightly after the operation, and were therefore slidden along by the trolleyful to men with needles and soldering irons, who vented them, and soldered the aperture. Except for the label, the "finest Columbia salmon" was ready for the market. — Rudyard Kipling, *American Notes* (1890; Boston: Brown and Co., 1899), 59–60

91. The machine as human: the "Iron Chink." This device, developed principally by E. A. Smith and first sold to a cannery in 1905, was essentially a large wheel that butchered and cleaned fish in a single revolution. Working at the rate of forty-five a minute, and later at sixty a minute, it processed as many fish in a day as ten Chinese had earlier done by hand. The machine was noisy, wasteful, and prone to throwing pieces of fish entrails around the cannery. Chinese labor, retained to operate the machine and to hand prepare fancy cuts of fish, disappeared from the Columbia River canneries only in the mid-1950s, when the industry itself made its last stand on the river. Courtesy Special Collections Division, University of Washington Libraries, A. Curtis no. 58196.

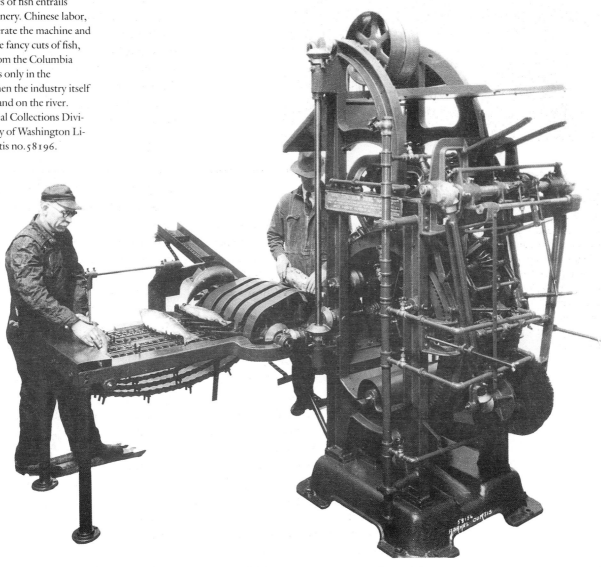

Labor's Many Faces

The history of the [metal] mining camp at Butte dates back nearly forty years to the early seventies. The labor supply at first was almost equally composed of Irish and English, with a scattering of Swedes, Norwegians, Germans, and native-born. These races were employed in varying proportions, with the Irish and English always most numerous, as they are to-day, until, late in the nineties, members of the Finnish, North Italian, and various Austrian races began to assume importance as elements in the labor supply. About the same time a small number of Greeks and Russians were also given employment. The Montenegrins had been added within the two years previous to the time of the investigation. Most of them came from construction work on the railroads. – United States Immigration Commission, *Report* (1911)

The English-speaking immigrants and Germans who have migrated to the Northwest have, for the most part, gone into occupations other than lumbering. The Scandinavians, on the other hand, have immigrated in large numbers and a good share of them have taken employment as common laborers in the lumber mills until such time as they could advance to skilled trades or get possession of land and engage in agriculture. For the years 1901 to 1908, no fewer than 22,918 entered the United States, giving Oregon and Washington as their destination. – United States Immigration Commission, *Report* (1911)

With the exception of Wyoming, where the Chinese who had been employed as construction laborers on the Union Pacific Railroad composed the early supply of mine labor, the [coal] mines of the West were first operated largely by natives and north Europeans, and especially immigrants from the British Isles. As the industry developed, however, more men were needed and were secured from the most available sources. Furthermore, the mine laborers of the older type were progressive. Many of them left mining for agricultural or more profitable industrial pursuits. When the anti-Chinese agitation caused most of that race to leave Wyoming, their places had to be filled. Moreover, a number of strikes in various localities have caused a displacement of races. Thus throughout the development of the industry there has been a constant shifting of races.

The vacancies resulting from these causes have been filled chiefly by men applying at the mines. These have come to be more and more from south and east European countries. Many of this newer type of immigrants have found their way west as members of construction gangs, or as section hands on the railroads, leaving this work when they reached the Rocky Mountain States. Many of the Japanese came from the railroad gangs of the Northwest into the more remunerative work of the mines. – United States Immigration Commission, *Report* (1911)

Mr. Lowman. Women work eight hours in the industries of this State except in those of the canning of meats, fish, and fruits, where they are permitted to work 10 hours. Cases have been brought where women worked more than 8 hours on some part of the canning industry, other than mere handling and incasing in tin of the raw material, and a conviction was had, showing that the State labor department is active in seeing that even technical violations are prohibited and punished. The law was new and was not thoroughly understood, or even this case would not have been necessary.

To state that conditions are immoral is a base slander on my neighbors' wives and children. It is considered a sort of picnic by a good many to whom it is unnecessary, not at all necessary, in fact, that they work for a living. They want to work in the canneries for a limited length of time attracted by the high wage.
– Testimony of Will A. Lowman, president of Puget Sound Salmon Canneries Association, before U.S. Commission on Industrial Relations, Seattle, Washington, August 1914

92. Workers at the Schade Brewing Company, Spokane, typified the all-male environment found in many workplaces in the New Northwest. Courtesy Eastern Washington State Historical Society, no.L85-48.3.

The Male West in 1900

Rank in United States	State	Single Males in Population (%) 15 years and Older
1	Wyoming	58.2
2	Montana	56.8
3	Nevada	53.1
4	Washington	50.4
5	Arizona	49.5
6	Idaho	49.3
7	Oregon	47.8
8	Colorado	44.0
9	New Mexico	36.9

Source: United States, Bureau of the Census, Histori-cal Statistics of the United States *(Washington, D.C., 1975).*

93. Chinese construction workers on the Northern Pacific Railroad in Washington's Green River gorge in 1885. Three years earlier, when the railroad extended its main line across the eastern part of the territory, it recruited fifteen thousand Chinese construction workers. Courtesy Idaho State Historical Society, no.71-204.0.

Ethnic Composition of Common Laborers on Pacific Northwest Railroads Spring and Summer 1909

	Oregon Railroad & Navigation Company	Oregon Short Line	Northern Pacific*	Great Northern*
Chinese	—	68	132	—
Japanese and Korean	397	779	444	215
East Indian	14	30	5	—
Greek	—	794	45	743
Italian	930 (includes Greek)	357	894	851
Mexican	—	3	—	—
Miscellaneous White	587	310	1,656	1,070

*The census was confined to Northern Pacific lines west of Paradise, Montana, and to the Great Northern's Spokane and Cascade divisions.

Source: United States Immigration Commission, Report, 61st Cong., 2d Sess., 1911, SD 633, vol.25, "Immigrants in Industries," 7.

94. Japanese laborers on a Milwaukee Road handcar near Butte, Montana, dressed up for the photographer. Early in the twentieth century, the editor of the Seattle *Union Record* warned that the New Northwest was again on the verge of conflict over the use of Asian labor. "Jim Hill [president of the Great Northern] will have Japs as yardmen, engineers, and conductors if a check is not put upon his career of greed." Other labor papers in the Pacific Northwest nodded in agreement. Railroad work was, however, only a way station for many Japanese in the New Northwest. "In recent years a comparatively large number of the Japanese who had worked for wages on the railroads and farming have leased land and are now farming on their own accounts," noted the United States Immigration Commission. *Report*, 61st Cong., 2d Sess., 1911, SD 633, vol.25, "Immigrants in Industries," 521. Courtesy Montana Historical Society.

95. Japanese merchant making a delivery in Port Blakely, Washington. This occupation represented a step up the economic ladder from the heavy physical labor that railway construction and maintenance demanded. To help prepare Oregon's Hood River valley to grow apples, landowners brought in Japanese laborers at the turn of the century. "The industrious Orientals stayed by the job. They dug out stumps, cut slashing, burned debris, tilled the soil, and transformed cut-over waste into a vast garden." But when Japanese laborers saved their earnings and bought orchard land of their own and built homes, they created resentment and prompted a state legislator from Hood River to introduce a bill prohibiting Asians from owning land in Oregon.
– *Oregon, End of the Trail* (Portland: Binfords & Mort, 1940), 79, 179. Courtesy Puget Sound Maritime Historical Society, no.4636-064.

96. Black workers helped to pave Riverside Avenue in Spokane about 1898. Until World War II, blacks constituted a smaller portion of the work force in the New Northwest than they did in any other region of the United States. The largest industrial employer of black labor in Washington from 1880 to 1900 was the coal industry, where several hundred blacks were lured west as strikebreakers by being told that they were needed to open new mines. A black community emerged in the coal town of Roslyn, west of Ellensburg, following strikes by white miners in 1888 and 1892.

Until World War II, trade unions effectively closed their doors to skilled black workers. Even after Pearl Harbor, when blacks in the aircraft and shipbuilding industries applied for union membership, tensions arose. At Boeing Aircraft, the union refused to admit blacks and in effect contributed to shaping company policy. In Portland's shipyards, the Boilermakers' Union segregated blacks into auxiliary unions. Blacks paid dues but had no vote in union matters, and when the war ended they found that their classification as temporary members gained them no seniority in the scramble for jobs. Courtesy Eastern Washington State Historical Society, no.L85-224.

Race in the Mills

Most of the mills, however, have not employed Japanese, and the prejudices against them have prevented them from being employed as extensively as they otherwise would have been. In some cases, they have not been employed because of the race prejudices of the employer, but in more numerous instances because of the attitude of the employees, who almost invariably dislike the Japanese. In one instance 50 Japanese brought from Portland were not permitted to leave the train. In a second where they, at a lower wage, replaced Italians, the Japanese found it difficult to live in the community. Evidences of hostility have been found elsewhere, but in most places they have not been open. Yet the antagonism has been effective in preventing the Japanese from gaining entrance to some of the mills and from finding employment, other than the least remunerative, in most of the mills where they have been employed. – *Source:* United States Immigration Commission, *Report,* 61st Cong., 2d Sess., 1911, SD 633, Vol.25, "Immigrants in Industries," 347

97. Indian hop pickers in Washington state in 1893. Native Americans could also be found in sawmills on Puget Sound. In the first steam-powered mill that opened in Seattle in 1853, they labored alongside white workers. Courtesy Eastern Washington State Historical Society, no.L84-393.89.

98. Hispanic harvest laborers in Oregon's Willamette Valley, probably during World War II. Compared to the Southwest, the New Northwest had relatively few Mexican and Mexican-American workers until the early 1940s. When the war created a shortage of agricultural labor, the United States government imported workers (*braceros*) directly from Mexico to the Pacific Northwest; at one time during the war, more than thirty-nine thousand Mexican males were employed in Oregon, Washington, and Idaho. Courtesy Oregon State University Archives, no.P20:518.

99. Construction scene in 1905 on the Mink Creek Canal, Cache Valley, Idaho. All of the men are identified on the back of the photograph by their first and last names, but the women are listed only as Liz and Bess. Courtesy Idaho State Historical Society, no.61-179.1.

100. Men and women share a moment together on the logging frontier. The photographer provided no record of the occasion, but it certainly was not a typical workday. Perhaps the presence of women in the woods was reason enough for a picture. Courtesy Photographic Archives, Museum of History and Industry, Seattle, no.9501.

101. Women workers in an apple-packing plant in the Spokane Valley, 1914. This was a scene repeated year after year in a number of different locales. "With the beginning of the cherry harvest, toward midsummer, Produce Row [in Yakima], always busy, becomes more hectic, and the narrow paved street is a shifting mass of trucks and shunting freight cars. Day and night the Row is a river of flowing traffic; gasoline fumes mingle with heavy odors of ripened fruit and the clank of hurried machinery. Above the roar of trucks and motors, the sounding of horns, and the shouts of drivers, rise the hoarse whistles of railroad locomotives and warning switch engine bells. In a mounting crescendo of industrial activity, peaches, pears, and apples follow each other in season. Overalled women clad in dull blue or gray uniforms, heads covered with close-fitting bonnets, crowd in increasing numbers into the various plants to care for the freshly gathered fruits hauled from thousands of acres of orchards in numberless trucks, horse-drawn wagons, family automobiles, and freight cars. Transient fruit workers, 'apple knockers' (packers), wives and daughters of near-by farmers and townspeople are drawn into service and labor at terrific speed." – *Washington, A Guide to the Evergreen State* (Portland: Binfords & Mort, 1941), 300. Courtesy Eastern Washington State Historical Society, no.L87-1.10854-14.

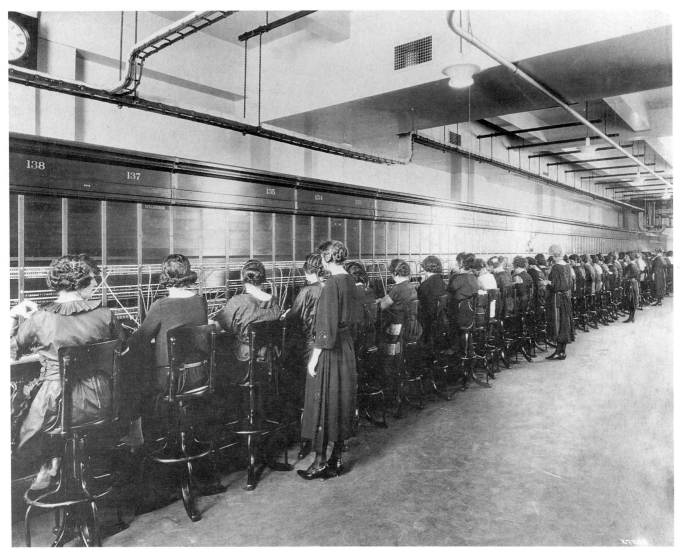

102. Telephone operators ("hello girls") in Seattle in the 1920s. Automated equipment would later reduce their numbers dramatically. A woman employed at a small exchange in Montana recalled, "It was every operator's dream that when her ship came in she would open all the keys on a busy board, yell 'To hell with you,' pull all the plugs and march out in triumph, leaving everything in total chaos. Nobody ever did. We felt an awful responsibility toward our little corner of the world. We really helped keep it running, one girl at a time all by herself at the board." – Dorothy M. Johnson, "Confessions of a Telephone Girl," in *The Last Best Place: A Montana Anthology,* ed. William Kittredge and Annick Smith (Helena: Montana Historical Society Press, 1988), 734. Courtesy Photographic Archives, Museum of History and Industry, Seattle, no. 17731.

103. On the "sausage line" at Carsterns in Tacoma in September 1924. Courtesy Tacoma Public Library, Northwest Room, no.245a.

104. Laundry workers in Spokane in 1928. Writers have detailed the "romance" of logging, mining, fishing, and farming, but no one ever claimed that work in a steam laundry was romantic. A census of laundry workers in Washington in 1909 listed 2,101 females and 1,135 males; in the other three states of the New Northwest, a similar ratio prevailed. Courtesy Eastern Washington State Historical Society, no.L87-1.37166.28.

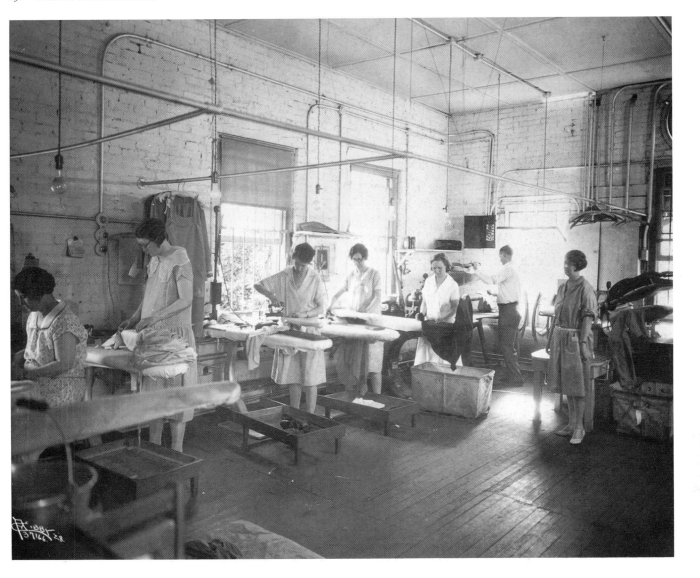

105. Rivet heaters and passers at
the Puget Sound Naval Shipyard,
Bremerton, in May 1919. Courtesy
National Archives, no.86-G111F-7

106. Waitresses from the Banquet Restaurant in Wallace, Idaho, posed as a chorus line in the mid-1920s. This was apparently the photographer's way to glamorize their work. The person behind the camera, incidentally, was Nellie Stockbridge, a professional photographer who recorded several decades of life in the Coeur d'Alene mining region.

Trained as a photographer in Chicago, she accepted a job with Thomas Nathan Barnard in 1898 and later acquired the Barnard Studio. Barnard himself had learned the trade from L. A. Huffman of Miles City, Montana, in the early 1880s. Courtesy Barnard-Stockbridge Collection, no.8-0772, University of Idaho Library.

107. Linotype operators in Burley, Idaho, in 1926. Because the machines used molten lead to form "slugs" of type vital to the printing industry, the work was hot and dirty; and if the liquid metal accidentally squirted onto the operator's legs, it could also be painful. Courtesy Idaho State Historical Society, no.79-37.5.

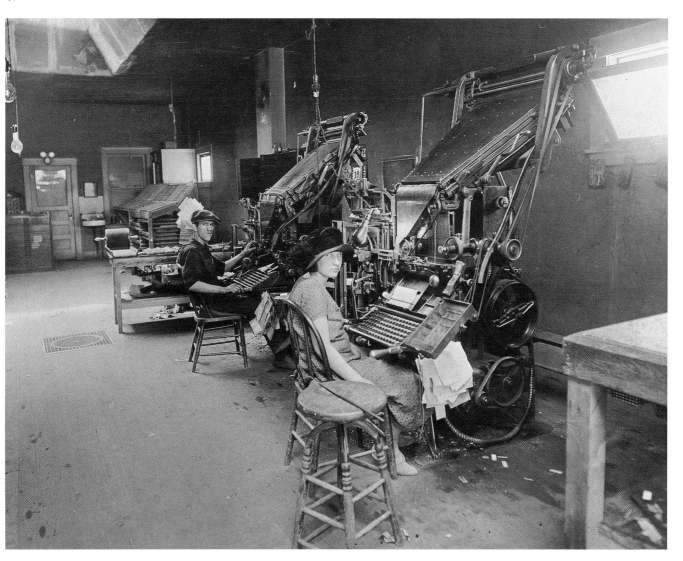

108. "Timberettes" on the green chain, Snoqualmie Falls Lumber Company. Women during World War II held a wide range of jobs in sawmills of the Pacific Northwest, confounding critics who charged that only husky men could do such work. These women pulled rough green lumber off a moving chain conveyor. Courtesy Forest History Society.

Cultural Diversity on Resurrection Day

On October 19, 1915, sixteen shift bosses and assistant foremen on surface for their lunch hour were grouped around the shaft of the Granite Mountain Mine [near Butte] awaiting the 12:30 whistle to announce the time for lowering the mine cage to take them down below to their work. Beside them on the surface turn-sheets a small hand-truck with twelve cases of forty-per cent dynamite also was waiting to be lowered.

At the first blast of the whistle, from a cause that has never been determined, the twelve boxes of powder exploded with a roar that could be heard for miles. The sixteen men standing around the shaft were blown to atoms. Fingers with rings attached were found a mile from the scene. Undertakers scoured the surrounding hills for days, seeking portions of the bodies. What they found was sealed in caskets and a combined public funeral was held.

Shortly after the explosion, several undertakers were engaged in searching for fragments of the victims' bodies. As small parts were found they were placed in one large basket. A well-known character, drawn to the scene with thousands of others, watched with morbid fascination.

"Hm-m-m," he commented to a bystander, "Puttin' 'em all together in one basket — Corkmen, Far-downs, Cousin Jacks, Democrats, Republicans, Masons, and Knights of Columbus. There's goin' to be a helluva mix-up there on Resurrection Day!" — *Copper Camp: Stories of the World's Greatest Mining Town, Butte, Montana*, comp. Writers' Program, Work Projects Administration (New York: Hastings House, 1943), 165

Worker Communities: Urban Islands and Hinterlands

Mr. Mack. At times we will perhaps run shy of common labor. . . . We phone up here [to an employment agency in Seattle] and ask if they can't send down such and such men. He probably sends 25 or 30 men, and they will be scattered between 8 or 10 different camps, you understand. This, Seattle, you understand, is the clearing house, this is the commercial center, and the labor is scattered over a large territory. The city of Seattle is one and Portland is another clearing house, the same way, for a good portion of Washington and all of Oregon. Aberdeen and Hoquiam are big lumber centers. There are over 2,000,000 feet per day of lumber manufactured, and some of the largest and best mills in the State are there. There is quite a demand for labor. But often when a man gets out of work he wants to have a high old time, and he comes to Seattle, and when he strikes the streets here you will find more unrest and more discontent in the labor district in Seattle than anywhere else in the State. It has become so flagrant that we almost hesitate to send for men here in the city of Seattle. You are liable to get out a lot of fellows like that that are more uneasy, discontented, and trouble breeders. – Testimony of William B. Mack, manager of S. E. Slade Lumber Company, before U.S. Commission on Industrial Relations, Seattle, Washington, August 1914

In this city [Portland] are 18 male employment agencies operated for private gain. If a man is in southern Oregon in search of work, he must come to a labor agency in Portland, even though the agency collects fees and sends the man back to a job in the district from which he came. In the Northwest, where the distances between industrial centers are so great, a man without work frequently has the alternative of consuming a large part of his income in traveling to the nearest industrial center or of resorting to the illegal practice of riding the freight cars. One course leads to destitution and the other to vagrancy. – A. E. Wood exhibit, presented to the U.S. Commission on Industrial Relations, Portland, Oregon, August 1914

So it was, in the old West, when news of a "job" was broadcast by press, wire, grapevine and mail. The hoboes and the Bohunks, engineers, mechanics, hard-rock men, teamsters and horses, machines, materials, food most imperishable, tools, work clothes, tobacco and snuff, selected sorts of people and things, converged from all points of the compass to form a community, achieve an end, and disperse. – Elliott Paul, *Desperate Scenery* (1954)

The city with the copper soul was built around
the mines of Butte. The people of this mining
camp breathed copper, ate copper, wore copper, and were thoroughly saturated with copper. The smoke, fumes and dust penetrated
everywhere. Many of the miners were suffer-
ing from rankling copper sores, caused by the
poisonous water. – William D. Haywood, *Bill
Haywood's Book* (1929), 82

109. Looking up Main Street in Burke, a mining camp located in the Bitterroot Mountains near Wallace, Idaho. A stampede of miners to the Coeur d'Alene district occurred during the winter and spring of 1883–84 when five thousand gold seekers scrambled to reach the diggings. Buoyed by the hope of sudden riches, they braved snowdrifts twenty feet deep in the mountain passes; they used toboggans and snowshoes, the only transportation available until the snow melted in April.

Miners at first used relatively simple and inexpensive placer methods to recover the gold. But with the discovery of silver on the south fork of the Coeur d'Alene River, the character of the rush changed dramatically because underground deposits of silver were far more difficult to mine than was gold on the surface. It required complex technology and large amounts of capital. Mining silver also demanded a large labor force that soon made Coeur d'Alene settlements like Burke resemble mining and industrial centers in Pennsylvania or West Virginia. Spokane, the main supply point for the Idaho mines, became the district's dominant urban center. Courtesy Haynes Foundation Collection, Montana Historical Society, Haynes no. 2995.

Like Blowing Out a Candle

Q. [Representative John C. Bell] Mining is your chief industry?
A. [T. N. Barnard, photographer in Wallace, Idaho] Yes; it is our only industry.
Q. All other vocations depend upon the success of the miners?
A. Exactly.
Q. If the mines shut down, it is like blowing out a candle, practically?
A. It is, I think, on the same principle.
— Report of the Industrial Commission on the Relations and Conditions of Capital and Labor Employed in the Mining Industry (1901), vol. 12, 415

Recollections of the Coeur d'Alene Stampede in 1884

Everywhere the trails leading from the "city" were lined with men bearing camp outfits and miners' tools on the way into the mountain fortresses, in search of the precious metal, and the excitement became epidemic, but one knew not which way to turn there were so many conflicting rumors in the district.

The little stores were packed with eager buyers, and the saloons and gambling halls were miniature pandemoniums of bustle and noise.

It was truly surprising to find very large stocks of goods kept in the crude log and canvas stores, comprising almost every article known to civilized lands, packed through drifts of snow across mountain ranges, and one could obtain many of the luxuries belonging to life in long settled communities, provided the state of the purse would admit.

Butter cost two to three dollars, potatoes one to two dollars, and beef and bacon two dollars per pound, eggs were worth one dollar each, and canned goods on the average twenty-five dollars per case. – A. H. Hersey in *Northwest Magazine* 4 (December 1886), 5

110. Life's amenities: a bakery delivered freshly baked bread to Coeur d'Alene miners in Idaho Territory in 1884. Spurring miners on in their dawn-to-dusk labors were advertisements proclaiming: "Nuggets weighing $50, $100, $200 of free gold for the picking up; it fairly glistens." Courtesy Haynes Foundation Collection, Montana Historical Society, Haynes no.1389.

111. Riverside Hotel, Hoquiam, Washington. This group of people was typical of the "economic families" living in the New Northwest at the turn of the century. The federal census recognized two types of families: natural and economic. The latter included dwellers in hotels, boardinghouses, institutions, and construction, timber, mining, and military camps. That is, an economic family defined people who lodged together but had no natural or private family relationship. – Courtesy Special Collections Division, University of Washington Libraries, uw no.2083.

112. Worker housing in Port Blakely. This settlement, which sprang to life in 1863 and soon became one of the leading lumber centers on Puget Sound, was typical of several sawmill towns on Washington's inland sea. Another was Port Gamble, a company town established in 1853 by Pope and Talbot. "No absentee owners were the Popes and Talbots who came around Cape Horn to build an industry. Long lines of shade trees grown from Maine elm slips still mark the original main street[,] and bright flower gardens set off the severe houses, in New England style. For their employees the owners built rows of box houses with steep-pitched roofs, then they added a company store, a community hall, and a church; finally, they topped this program with a large hotel." – *Washington, A Guide to the Evergreen State* (Portland: Binfords & Mort, 1941), 573. Courtesy Historical Photograph Collections, Washington State University Libraries.

Economic Families, 1900 by Percentage of Population

Wyoming	15.6
Montana	15.3
Washington	13.8
Nevada	11.6
Arizona	11.2
California	11.1
Oregon	10.1
Colorado	8.0
Idaho	7.4
Utah	3.4
New Mexico	3.1
United States	3.4

Source: Twelfth Census of the United States: 1900 *Supplementary Analysis and Derivitive Tables (Washington, D.C.: Government Printing Office, 1906), 376–79 passim.*

Counterpoint: Industrial Feudalism

In a typical saw mill town, industrial feudalism exists in its worst form. The lumber company, by reason of its economic control, is the one supreme power. Usually the local political office holders are either employees of the company, or are economically dependent on it in some way, and thus completely under its control. The entire life of the community revolves around the saw mill. The workers in the saw mill live in company owned houses, or board at the company boarding house. They trade at the company store; their children go to a company controlled school; when they are sick they go to the company hospital, or are treated by the company doctor. When they are dead they are buried in the company cemetery, and their souls are saved by a company preacher. – James Rowan, *The I. W. W. in the Lumber Industry* (Seattle: Lumber Workers Industrial Union no. 500 [192?]), 7

Mill Work

The mill is a black frame shed, 300 feet long and 150 feet wide. Catwalks afford a safe view of the screeching, bellowing room; danger signs warn against going near the whirring machines. The logs, sawed into convenient lengths before they leave the woods, are hooked out of the pond in the rear of the plant by an endless belt, set with ugly sharp prongs, that carries them to the three saw carriages; band saws on pulleys rip through them. Sawdust is carried off to the engine room where it feeds the big furnaces that generate steam to operate the machines. Endless chains carry the boards to the planing departments where they are smoothed or made into shingles and lath; or to other departments for special treatment. On the top floor of the shed is the filing room, where band saws are filed mechanically. All over the mill the men work fast; they wear clothing without loose ends. The noise seems unbearable to newcomers. – description of the Bonner mill from *Montana, A State Guide Book* (New York: Viking Press, 1939), 311

113. The photographer Wesley Andrews preserved on film this image of a large sawmill in Elk River, Idaho. "Elk River stood virtually in hole cut out of a dense forest cover of mature white pine," one resident recalled. It was in many ways typical of the several dozen milltowns scattered throughout western Montana, northern Idaho, and eastern Washington. Another of them was Potlatch, Idaho, located about fifty miles northwest of Elk River. It dated from 1905 when the Potlatch Lumber Company constructed more than 250 buildings on hills that overlooked the largest white pine sawmill in the world. At one time, two thousand people lived in the bustling community that could boast an opera house, paved streets, and wooden sidewalks. But the mill closed in 1981, and many sawmill workers left. A way of life had ended. It was a pattern that occurred in Elk River and numerous other natural resource–based communities of the region. Courtesy Oregon Historical Society, no.34042.

114. The waterfront in Everett, Washington, "City of Smokestacks," was one of the principal nerve centers of the state's timber industry and a busy lumber port. The lumber and shingle mills here were large permanent installations that employed mostly local workers. The city's air was heavy with the smell of cedar and spruce, and residents everywhere set their clocks and watches by the mill whistles. Courtesy Special Collections Division, University of Washington Libraries, A. Curtis, no.28875.

115. One of labor's temporary communities: a "wanigan" photographed on Idaho's Clearwater River. It followed the log drive and functioned as a portable camp; this one contained the vital cookhouse. The word originated among the loggers of Maine and traveled west with the logging frontier. Courtesy Forest History Society.

116. Life aboard a "wanigan" during the Clearwater log drive of May 1941. Logs were floated down other rivers – including the Kootenai, Flathead, and Priest – to sawmills of the New Northwest. Even creeks played a role in the spring drives when splash dams were used to create brief floods to float logs downstream. The men who worked the log drives were often known as river pigs. Courtesy Eastern Washington State Historical Society, no.L85-143.204.

117. Seattle's Pioneer Square as seen by Asahel Curtis in April 1904. Its chief landmark until 1939 was the 140-year-old totem pole brought to Seattle in 1889. "The 'square' is a small triangular plot, graced with a green pavilion above the entrance to a men's lavatory, and surrounded by flophouses, pawnshops, beer parlors, loggers' employment agencies, offices of quack doctors, and outfitters for Alaska and the lumber camps. Still known as the Skidroad, the district is thronged with men of all races and occupations – lumberjacks in town for a few weeks, fisherman back from Alaska, sailors on leave or in search of a ship, wandering farm laborers, boys far from home, drifters, cripples, beggars. Indians from out of the city make a habit of meeting in the square. Knots of men form around arguments concerning politics, religion, economics; and street speakers and the Salvation Army carry on their work." *Washington, A Guide to the Evergreen State* (Portland: Binfords & Mort, 1941), 224–25. Courtesy Washington State Historical Society, A. Curtis no.4630.

118. A logging camp on the Stillaguamish River near Arlington, Washington, at the turn of the century. "Although it once ranked with the largest shingle manufacturing centers, Arlington now [in the late 1930s] has only one mill and, like many other western Washington towns, has turned to dairying, poultry-raising, truck-gardening, and fruit growing." – *Washington, A Guide to the Evergreen State* (Portland: Binfords & Mort, 1941), 478. Courtesy Special Collections Division, University of Washington Libraries, UW no.10628.

Bunkhouse Life

The worst thing I find that the men in the logging camps have to contend with is the bad conditions. There is one logging camp on Grays Harbor where they have a bunk house with room in the bunk house for about 50 persons. Those men sleep in wooden bunks; those bunks are double tiers running clear around the building. Those bunk houses have only one window in one end of them. A man would have to light a lamp to read in the middle of the day. They have a big stove in the center of that, and the only other comfort is a bench that runs around on a level with the lower bunk. A man can sit on those benches, or per-

haps have a box or something of that sort to sit on if they want to sit around the table and play cards or something of that character. They have stoves, and in the periods of the year when it is raining the stoves are hung all about with wet clothing. That is their only method that these loggers and woodmen have of drying their clothes. The men naturally in the bunks have to inhale the steam that comes off of these drying clothes. – Testimony of J. G. Brown, president of the International Union of Timber Workers, Seattle, Washington, August 1914. *Report of the Commission on Industrial Relations,* 64th Cong., 1st Sess., 1916, Senate Document 415, vol.5, p.4211

A First-Class Skidroad Saloon

In the first-class skidroad saloon the logger
was treated like a gentleman as long as he con-
ducted himself like one; there he could feel like
a free-born American citizen – as long as he
was a customer. Going broke, the illusion
ended. But it had been grand while it lasted,
and he always looked forward to its repetition
when he was toiling his ten or 12 hours a day
in the woods again. – James Stevens,
"Skidroad Palaces," *Four L Lumber News* 9
(April 1, 1927), 6

119. Darius Kinsey photographed
bunkhouse life in the Washington
woods. Courtesy Special Collections Division, University of Washington Libraries, D. Kinsey
no.155-A.

120. Christie's Saloon in Troy,
Idaho, in the early 1900s was no
Erickson's, but it was probably typi-
cal of the drinking establishments
frequented by workers in small
towns of the New Northwest.
Courtesy Latah County Historical
Society, no.15-3-8.

Y.M.C.A. LIBRARY AT FIRDALE WASH.

121. YMCA public library in Firdale, Washington, in 1912. A special kind of worker sanctuary was the permanent library or reading room where "the principal progressive papers will be on file." This room, suggested a labor reformer in the mid-1880s, "should be made comfortable and attractive so as to lead the members to patronize it instead of a saloon; and were a coffee room attached it might be made profitable." The need for a library to cater to the interests of labor was all the more urgent at a time when public libraries were generally not open at hours convenient for workers who were on the job ten to twelve hours a day. Courtesy Special Collections Division, University of Washington Libraries, A. Curtis no.25305.

122. The DeLamar miners' band, circa 1900. The musicians' home community, a once prosperous mining town located nine miles from Silver City, Idaho, was deserted by the 1930s, "though down the long winding main street many of the buildings still stand, smelling of emptiness and death. In the second-story parlor of the hotel, the piano strings have been taken by rust; and upon the window ledges of the assay office there are dusty bottles and the smell of acid. The footprints upon the streets now are those of the rabbit and the coyote." –*Idaho, A Guide in Word and Picture* (Caldwell: Caxton Printers, 1937), 384–85. Courtesy Idaho State Historical Society, no.77-147.1.

Feeling the Music

A leading feature of this date at the Interstate Fair is that it is Miners' day. The miners from the towns east of Tacoma did the day honor. The intelligent and robust people from Carbonado, Franklin, Roslyn, South Prairie and other towns came into the city this morning in very large numbers. . . .

The Carbonado brass band was one of the attractions of the day, in its unique uniform, and it is a good band, too, as the many thousands who heard it play will testify. . . . The boys wore light brown canvas caps with miners' lamps above the peaks. Their shirts were dark blue flannel, and light blue overalls, red belts and canteens completed the uniform. The drum major was a most conspicuous and lively person. He can give lots of other drum majors in this State pointers on wielding the "club." He kept it the air from the station to Ninth street, and never allowed it to touch the earth. His shirt was red—so red you could feel it.

— Tacoma *News,* Sept. 29, 1894, p.1

Pastures of Plenty

FOLIO 5

Mr. Marsh. It strikes me that we need Federal aid in the matter of land development, the matter of placing people upon the land. The land question is too great for me to go into at any length. But let me tell you and assure you, Mr. Chairman, that in this city, and I think it is typical all over the State, that the longing for a piece of land is in the hearts of the people. They want a piece of land, but it is held by speculators out of their reach. The time was when a man could come West, as he was displaced in the East, and settle down on a piece of land. You can not do it to-day. — Testimony of E. P. Marsh, Washington State Federation of Labor president, before U.S. Commission on Industrial Relations, Seattle, Washington, August 1914

Mr. Page. Right here at the back door of Seattle we have the valley of the Puyallup, the White, the Black, and the Green Rivers. That is probably as rich land as anywhere in the world. For all practical purposes for years this land has lain idle. Some has been used, but there was a great deal idle. There is a great deal idle now. We have had these unemployed men walking the railroad tracks back and forth through this land for years and they haven't done anything with it. In the last few years the little Jap man came in. He paid thirty to forty dollars cash rent for that land in advance, and he farmed it and farmed it for a few years and takes the proceeds and goes back to Japan an independent man; and the Japanese cousin or brother or uncle comes and steps on the rented land and does the same thing and repeats it. The inclination to go on the land is there and he takes the land, and the fellow that is walking the railroad tracks with the bundle of blankets on his back has the same opportunity, but he hasn't got the inclination. — Testimony of Paul E. Page, president of Page Lumber Company, before U.S. Commission on Industrial Relations, Seattle, Washington, August 1914

Mr. Thompson. What is your opinion of the condition of labor here [in Portland] in the various industries, or in your particular industry, if you are more particularly acquainted with one?

Mr. Burchard. Well, I don't consider them very good.

Mr. Thompson. What is the reason? What industry? Perhaps you would rather particularize. What industry have you more in mind?

Mr. Burchard. Well, to begin with, business is quiet in all industries. The fact of the matter is, there is no business. But men keep flocking in just the same. And the more men come, the less business there is. The country in my estimate is overflooded with Greeks, Slavonians, Italians, and things of that sort, people who have no idea of what they are brought here for, or any thing of that kind. They are used like cattle after they get here.

Mr. Thompson. Do you think there is too much immigration, that that is one of the causes of unrest?

Mr. Burchard. Yes

Mr. Thompson. Now, what is the cause of immigration, if you have any idea on that.

Mr. Burchard. Cutting wages, perhaps.

Mr. Thompson. I mean what causes people to come here?

Mr. Burchard. Why, I think they are brought here by alluring literature. I have an idea from the reports that can be gathered, that that is what bought them here.

– Testimony of T. H. Burchard, Oregon State Federation of Labor president, Central Labor Council of Portland and Vicinity president, and musician by trade, before U.S. Commission on Industrial Relations, Portland, Oregon, August 1914

Commercial clubs, the State immigration commission, and railroad companies send broadcast pamphlets about the opportunities in Oregon. Doubtless the purpose of this advertising is to attract persons who have sufficient capital to make an economic success; nevertheless it is an incontestable fact that these publications reach hundreds of workingmen who have nothing to offer but their labor and who are misled by the inexplicit and vague phrases of the advertisers. Once here they may come to realize, though only too late, that as wage earners they meet with the same fluctuating conditions of employment in Oregon as elsewhere. – A. E. Wood exhibit, presented to the U.S. Commission on Industrial Relations, Portland, Oregon, August 1914

123. The enduring lure of the land: from the early irrigation projects of the mid-nineteenth century until the Columbia Basin Project seen here in the years after World War II, couples dreamed of making the desert bloom. Beginning in the late 1940s, the waters impounded by Grand Coulee Dam were raised by a complex system of pumps and siphons to irrigate this vast stretch of semiarid land in central Washington. For decades, the promise of such land had been that it would solve the nation's "labor question." The Seattle *Daily Telegraph* succinctly expressed this popular notion when it editorialized in 1894: "All social problems solve themselves in the presence of a boundless expanse of vacant fertile land." That same year the Los Angeles *Times* advised, "If Congress would only get through squabbling over the tariff and the income tax and spend some weeks devising a plan for irrigating what is now worthless land, they would go a long way toward settling the labor difficulties which now confront us."

Among members of Coxey's Army, the masses of unemployed who marched on Capitol Hill that year to demand help during the worst depression the nation had yet experienced, was a man from San Francisco who no doubt spoke for many workers in the West. He explained to a public gathering in Saint Louis how federal dollars could help the jobless to realize the western dream of individual opportunity by putting them to work building the vast irrigation systems necessary to bring water to arid lands. "When the ditches are dug and the lands reclaimed we can register homestead claims and be self-supporting ever after."

That sounded too much like the ending to a fairy tale, and for most workers it was. As the Omaha *Bee* observed, "The problem of the city poor will have to be solved on the spot where it is found. The city poor must be relieved in the cities; they cannot be enabled to work out their own salvation for themselves by merely transporting some of them to a less densely populated soil." Courtesy Oregon Historical Society, no. 79631.

124. Milner, Idaho, on the opening day of the land office for the Twin Falls Irrigated Tract in 1909. This Carey Act project was one reason Idaho became a showcase for the irrigation measure passed by Congress in 1894. It embodied the dream of western members of Coxey's Army, who marched to Capitol Hill that same year believing that "the laboring man who cannot get the price which he considers his work to be worth can become a farmer, be his own master and become independent." Courtesy Utah State University Special Collections and Archives, no.A-3486.

125. Opening land from the Flathead Indian Reservation in Montana to settlement by non–Native Americans early in the twentieth century. William D. Haywood was one of the western workers who acquired former Indian reservation land at the turn of the century: "My farm was just below the old army post [Fort McDermitt, Nevada], where the valley was widest. We built foundations on the three places, and went to Winnemucca for lumber, out of which I built a one room house with a lean-to kitchen. This room I lined with burlap and whitewashed it. It made a fine wall and ceiling as tight as a drum. I moved my wife and baby down into the new house. Life began to take on a new aspect: every tap of work I did, building fences, digging ditches, was all for ourselves." – William D. Haywood, *Bill Haywood's Book* (New York: International Publishers, 1929), 41. Courtesy Montana Historical Society, no.950-741.

Wage Labor as Social Security

But now it was 1913 and the glittering prize of free land had stirred my father, as it had beckoned to hundreds of thousands of other Americans. Land for the asking! Land for the taking! No nation, no government in all history had ever offered its citizens such a bonanza.

My father, together with my mother's father and Grandpa's brother, formed a loose compact to claim 960 acres of land. Consequently, my father left his employment with the Northern Pacific Railroad as a railroad telegrapher to reap his fortune from the land. He had journeyed to Saco [Montana] and to the ranch site early in 1913 to help Grandpa construct a rude house which would shelter us until time and profit might permit the building of the grand ranch house. . . .

The weather turned adverse in 1916. . . . We were now engaged in a brutal and soul-crushing struggle for survival. . . . Drought, locusts, rust, Russian thistle, hail, and assorted reversals had depleted not only our capital but the spirit of my parents and grandparents. . . . Through the ranch years Dad maintained his "license" as a railroad telegrapher. Once in a while the Great Northern would be in desperate need of a temporary telegrapher to fill in for a regular employee who was ill. Consequently, Dad could usually secure "passes" or free transportation for the family. . . .

Dad now began to return to railroading, but still on a part-time basis, working what was called the "second trick," from four in the afternoon until midnight, seven days a week. He invested in an automobile . . . one of Henry Ford's earlier models. Whatever its capricious character, and it had that in generous measure, it carried Dad back and forth, from ranch to town. The check from the Great Northern, twice per month, was more money than my parents had seen in several years! – Chet Huntley, *The Generous Years* (New York: Random House, 1968), 10–61 *passim*

126. Homesteading in the forest near Tillamook, Oregon. Courtesy Oregon Historical Society, no. 2639.

The Homesteading Worker

In 1904, while living in Oregon, I decided to take up a homestead. The great wave of homesteaders, so basic in the settling of the West, was then wearing itself out. There was still much government free land, but the fertile prairies and valleys were long since taken. . . . Our locality [near the Hood River Valley] was inspiring country in which to spend a few months yearly in the spring and summer, which was all the homestead laws required. I earned my way by working in logging camps or on railroad jobs in the surrounding country, and I had no idea of ceasing to be an industrial worker. – William Z. Foster, *Pages from a Worker's Life* (New York: International Publishers, 1939), 30–31

127. Burning stumps from logged-off lands near Sumner, Washington. "Wherever the big timber is cleared – and many of the farms are abandoned logging camps – there is found the richest soil imaginable. It raises hay, potatoes, oats, barley, wheat, hops, cherries, apples, berries, and all which that list implies. It is a natural grazing land. The grass is forever green, and cattle and sheep keep 'hog-fat all the year,'" or so held the myth that Julian Ralph helped to perpetuate in his 1893 account *Our Great West* (New York: Harper & Brothers, 1893), 304.

The WPA guide to Washington, published almost half a century later, offered a much more truthful assessment when it recalled the history of the land around Usk, in the state's northeastern corner. "Rapidly logging operations ate into the forests, leaving behind large areas of stump lands, which were then offered at about ten or twelve dollars an acre. Land-hungry men and women, seeing the possibility of realizing the American dream, bought, cleared, and attempted to farm this land, little realizing that it cost from one to three hundred dollars to clear a single acre. Even when cleared the land was often unproductive, because of its gravel or clay composition.

"Many families moved elsewhere; those who remained, disheartened and disillusioned, struggled on, trying to make a living by growing potatoes and forage crops, selling milk and butter, and if any trees remained, by cutting cordwood, frequently the farmer's best crop. Much of the land around Usk is now cleared of farmers and will be returned to the status of timber land." *Washington, A Guide to the Evergreen State* (Portland: Binfords & Mort, 1941), 430. Courtesy Historical Photograph Collections, Washington State University Libraries, no.78-102.

Stumped by a Stump Ranch

Most of the settlers who will consider leaving their land during "good times" have not become sufficiently attached to the soil to want to spare a portion of their earnings to pay off the mortgage on it. Consequently, many of the industrial workers and other migrants coming to the Inland Empire during the last year have been able to buy land on which a goodly portion of the first toilsome labor of a stump ranch has already been expended, but with only a slightly larger outlay of money than the original purchaser made. – Nelle Portrey Davis, *Stump Ranch Pioneer* (New York: Dodd, Mead, 1942), 219

128. "HAVE FAITH IN GOD AND U.S. RECLAMATION." Russell Lee recorded this sign in Canyon County, Idaho, in May 1941. Irrigation was never merely a matter of digging ditches and transforming sagebrush deserts into farmland; it was widely perceived in the West as a type of social reform. When Congress passed the Newlands Act in 1902 it not only provided for the transformation of arid lands but also created thousands of construction jobs across the West. The measure explicitly stated that on Newlands projects the workday was to be eight hours and that no Asian labor might be employed. Courtesy Library of Congress, no.15761 LC-USF34 39242 Q.

129. A deserted farm west of Moses Lake, Washington, circa 1940. The WPA guide to Washington commented in the late 1930s, "This part of the Columbia Basin is both a land of promise and a graveyard of hope. Despite the lightness of the precipitation, which is seldom more than six inches annually, there are productive farms and flourishing stock ranches on the deep soil, rich in nitrates, lime, and magnesium. Scattered along the highway are ghost farms with their deserted houses, weather-beaten barns, and uprooted skeletons of fruit trees, a tragic residue left by settlers, who, at the turn of the century, hopefully broke the land and waited for the promised irrigation to materialize. The dream which they dreamed too soon is now about to become a reality." *Washington, A Guide to the Evergreen State* (Portland: Binfords & Mort, 1941), 330. Courtesy Eastern Washington State Historical Society, no.L85-143.367.

130. An Arthur Rothstein photograph from Oneida County, Idaho, in May 1936. The pamphlet in the man's hand is titled *Better Land for Better Living* and suggests the enduring dream of land as social security. Courtesy Library of Congress, no.LC-USF34-4630-D.

The New Deal and the Free-Land Safety Valve

Franklin D. Roosevelt in his last year at Harvard took a course called "American History: The Development of the West" under Frederick Jackson Turner. There was more than a hint of Turner's influence in Roosevelt's 1932 campaign speech to the Commonwealth Club of San Francisco, when he observed:

A glance at the situation today only too clearly indicates that equality of opportunity as we have known it no longer exists. Our industrial plant is built; the problem just now is whether under existing conditions it is not over-built. Our last frontier has long since been reached, and there is practically no more free land. More than half our people do not live on the farms or on lands and cannot derive a living by cultivating their own property. There is no safety valve in the form of a Western prairie to which those thrown out of work by the Eastern economic machines can go for a new start. — *Franklin D. Roosevelt: Selected Speeches, Messages, Press Conferences, and Letters,* ed. Basil Rauch (New York: Rinehart & Co., 1957), 81

Organize!

Mr. Thompson. Is any part of your establishment organized?

Mr. Mack. You mean labor?

Mr. Thompson. I mean labor.

Mr. Mack. No sir, not that I know of. We probably have quite a number of union men working. We never ask a man his religion, his politics, nor any of his beliefs.

Mr. Thompson. How do you personally view organized labor?

Mr. Mack. I am naturally opposed to it.

– Testimony of William B. Mack, manager of S. E. Slade Lumber Company, before U.S. Commission on Industrial Relations, Seattle, Washington, August 1914

Mr. Thompson. Has the fact that there is another organization [Industrial Workers of the World] seeking to organize the workers in the lumber industry affected the attitude of the employers toward your organization?

Mr. Brown. Well, I don't know. Outside of the shingle manufacturers – some of them we have had very friendly relations with for a long while – I have never met a man who in the logging and sawmill branches of the industry expressed a willingness to see his men organized in any kind of a union.

– Testimony of J. G. Brown, International Union of Timber Workers president, before U.S. Commission on Industrial Relations, Seattle, Washington, August 1914

Mr. Brown. I think the fact that the employer knows by merely telephoning to an industrial center he can get other men on the next train it makes him less patient with the men for any reason, be it frivolous or important, and he discharges the men because he knows he can get more to take their place very readily. That is one reason why the men change around so much. On the other hand, the fact that a man knows he can go and buy a job probably makes him less likely to stay in one place. . . . There are so many mills here where they will not simply allow the men to organize at all. Some mills even compel men to sign a statement before entering their employ, and they require them to sign a statement that they are not now, and will not during their employment with the firm, become a member of any labor organization. – Testimony of J. G. Brown, International Union of Timber Workers president, before U.S. Commission on Industrial Relations, Seattle, Washington, August 1914

131. The shop crew of the Oregon Short Line in Montpelier, Idaho, in 1905. The response of railroad workers to management as well as to long hours and dangers in the workplace was organization. Locomotive engineers were among the first workers in the New Northwest to form craft unions, in some cases as early as the 1870s. Typically, in recognition of their special status as railroad workers they called their organizations brotherhoods and held aloof from close association with other trade unions. Courtesy Idaho State Historical Society, no.65-99.60

132. Shop workers, Sprague, Washington Territory, April 1887. The railroad industry was in many ways a business pioneer, especially when growing size and complexity forced it to devise new ways to govern numerous employees scattered across a large area. To that end, railroads established an elaborate new type of managerial hierarchy adapted at least indirectly from the military. Not only were railroaders, particularly the operating crews, subject to close supervision and irregular hours, but their jobs were often as dangerous as any found off the battlefield. The Interstate Commerce Commission found that during the year that ended on June 30, 1893, 2,727 railroad workers were killed and another 31,729 injured in the line of duty. One of every 320 employees was killed that year, with the greatest number of deaths occurring while coupling or uncoupling cars. The all-time high accident rate among railroad workers occurred in 1907, when one of every eight engineers, firemen, conductors, and brakemen was injured on the job. Courtesy Montana Historical Society, Haynes no.1811.

As Deadly as War

Railroading is more nearly akin to warfare than any other human profession. The number of casualties to persons on our railways for the year ending June 30, 1907, was 122,855, of which 11,839 represented the number of persons killed and 111,016 the number injured. Of this number the passengers killed were 610 and those injured 13,041. The personal injuries, fatal and non-fatal, assume much the same aspect to the general officers in charge of a railway as to the general officers in command of an army. The responsibility of the railway officer, however, is greater, for he has not the excuse of war. — W. L. Park, general superintendent of the Union Pacific Railroad, in *Railroad Age Gazette,* Feb. 19, 1909, p.354

133. Members of the Miners' Union were photographed in Ketchum, Idaho, in the mid-1880s. In 1884 miners at Broadford and Bellevue organized a union to prevent employers from trimming fifty cents from their wages of four dollars a day. Industrial organization of western miners occurred initially in Central City, Colorado; Virginia City, Nevada; Silver City, Idaho; and several other camps during the 1860s. Courtesy Idaho State Historical Society, no.78-156.8.

134. Members of the Brick, Tile, and Terra Cotta Alliance march in Boise's Labor Day parade in 1903. Brickmaking became an important activity in the 1880s and 1890s when cities of the New Northwest switched from wood to more durable and fire-resistant building materials. Courtesy Idaho State Historical Society, no.79-71.5.

Labor's Patriotic Holiday

Conconully [Washington] celebrated Labor Day as patriotically and as enthusiastically in proportion to her population as did any of the numerous cities throughout the United States, nearly every one of which observed the custom. We did not have a big turnout of labor organizations in a procession headed by a brass band – because there is not more than one labor organization in this country and that is a good many miles away, and our band boys had not yet received their instruments – but we had drilling contests, horse racing, athletic sports, a picnic at the falls and a big dance at Woodmen hall in the evening – a pretty fair showing for our enterprising little city. Labor day is to the patriotic union working man what the Fourth of July is to the patriotic citizen. – *Okanagan Record,* Sept. 9, 1904, p.1

135. A Labor Day parade down Spokane's Riverside Avenue circa 1903. At this time a variety of trades had been organized in the city, but Spokane remained a magnet for the migratory laborer who typified the wageworkers' frontier. The Knights of Labor continued to be influential in Spokane until the opening years of the twentieth century, a bit longer than in most areas of the United States. Courtesy Eastern Washington State Historical Society, no.238.

36. The Seattle Newsboys Union.
Apart from newspaper boys, there
were relatively few child workers in
the New Northwest. In 1909 when
the region's manufacturing and
mining industries recorded a total
of 150,310 employees, only 461 of
them were children under age sixteen. Courtesy Special Collections
Division, University of Washington
Libraries, A. Curtis no.2849.

37. The Stone Masons Union in
Spokane about 1890, a time when
the city was feverishly rebuilding after the great fire of the previous
year. Courtesy Eastern Washington
State Historical Society,
no.L83-113.97.

38. A friendly game of baseball
pitted electricians against streetcar
men in Spokane's Natatorium Park
in 1901. Courtesy Eastern Washington State Historical Society,
no.7857.

139. Miners at the Trade Dollar Mine in Silver City, Idaho, in May 1900. William D. Haywood, recording secretary of the local Western Federation of Miners and later the embodiment of the militant Industrial Workers of the World, sits in profile on the front row, fourth from the right. Although places like Silver City were physically isolated, they were by no means cut off from the world of ideas. A reader from Silver City (in 1896) reported to the *Firebrand,* a Portland anarchist newspaper, that local miners were afraid that they might lose their jobs if they took out personal subscriptions to the journal; nonetheless, they read and passed around dog-eared copies. Whether one such reader was Haywood, he does not say. Haywood's career as a labor leader dated from 1896 in Silver City when Ed Boyce initiated him as a charter member of Local 66, Western Federation of Miners. Courtesy Idaho State Historical Society, no.596.

140. Wobblies pose outside the Arlington, Washington, branch of the Lumber Workers' Industrial Union no.500. Courtesy Archives of Labor and Urban Affairs, Wayne State University.

Frisco Mine Group

On April 29, 1899, a big demonstration was held at Wardner. All the members of all the unions in the district were there. The last warning had been sounded. The fuses were lit. Three thousand pounds of dynamite exploded. The Bunker Hill and Sullivan mill was blown up, ripped and smashed, a mass of twisted steel, iron and splintered timbers. The miners had released their pent-up resentment. There may have been some who regretted the destruction of that which workers had built, but the constraint of the entire population was for the time-being relieved. — William D. Haywood, *Bill Haywood's Book* (1929)

"Dump the Bosses off Your Back"
(Tune: "Take It to The Lord In Prayer")
Are you poor, forlorn and hungry?
　　Are there lots of things you lack?
Is your life made up of misery?
　　Then dump the bosses off your back.
Are your clothes all patched and tattered?
　　Are you living in a shack?
Would you have your troubles scattered?
　　Then dump the bosses off your back.
— *Songs of the Workers* (1973)

These newcomers took little part in politics; they were nomad labor, deprived of lawful vote. If this floating population voted at all, it was at the behest and with the illegal connivance of politicians who paid for their ballots. As such they became a "menace to good citizens." Yet they were true Americans, truer than most of the settled citizenry. They were direct inheritors of the fighting pioneer. Like him they were men of brawn and daring, proud of their strength to fell the forest, drive the new railroad, reclaim the trackless waste. They did these things no longer for their own homes on the frontier, but under order of railroad and lumber kings. Into their ballads there crept the bitter irony of men who "build all the homes of the world, and never have home [sic] of their own." They called their IWW hall the "home of the homeless." — Anna Louise Strong, *I Change Worlds* (1935)

141. A photograph from the 1894 Pullman strike in Billings, Montana, vividly illustrates how labor disputes in the New Northwest in the late nineteenth and early twentieth centuries sometimes resembled a state of war. Courtesy Montana Historical Society, Northern Pacific File.

142. The Rock Springs Massacre. The spark that touched off the first major episode of industrial violence in the New Northwest occurred in the coal-mining town of Rock Springs, Wyoming, where racial tension had mounted steadily after the Union Pacific Railway successfully resisted efforts by the Knights of Labor to force Chinese workers out of its company mines. A mob of white miners on September 2, 1885, wantonly attacked the Chinese, drove them from Rock Springs, and in the brutal process killed twenty-eight and wounded fifteen.

Less than a week later, news of such events inspired a small group of whites and Indians to murder three Chinese hop pickers in Washington's Squak Valley east of Seattle. Four days after that, at the Newcastle mines of the Oregon Improvement Company, one of the largest and most powerful coal operators in the territory, a dozen masked men set fire to the quarters where thirty-seven Chinese workers slept. They escaped but lost all their belongings in the blaze. The next day the Chinese fled the Newcastle area. Throughout the New Northwest, white workers were in a state of agitation that culminated in the expulsion of Chinese from Tacoma, violence in Seattle, and martial law. Courtesy Union Pacific Railroad Museum Collection, Omaha, no. 502112.

143. L. A. Huffman photographed Coxey's Army in camp at Forsyth, Montana, in April 1894. These men, mostly metal miners, attracted nationwide attention when they stole a train in Butte and headed east to present a living petition to Congress to do something about the severe depression wracking the nation. Followed by a trainload of federal marshals, they steamed rapidly over the backbone of the Rockies at Homestake Pass and eastward on the Northern Pacific line through Bozeman and into Billings, where townspeople sympathetic to the unemployed drove the marshals back in a bloody confrontation. On the plains near Miles City, the episode ended as abruptly as it had begun with a peaceful surrender to the United States Army. In all, fifty or more cases of train stealing by unemployed Americans occurred during a desperate two-month period in the spring of 1894.

Cycles of boom-and-bust typified the New Northwest's early economic growth, but the worst of the pre-1930s depressions lasted from 1893 to 1897. The resulting misery was unprecedented, as workers lost jobs, farmers saw prices fall below the cost of production, and depositors saw banks collapse and their savings evaporate. Along the shores of Puget Sound, people built driftwood shanties and subsisted on clams and other edibles. When in the spring of 1894 an Ohioan named Jacob Coxey announced that he was going to lead an army of the unemployed to Capitol Hill to call for temporary public works jobs, hundreds of idle workers in Seattle, Tacoma, and Spokane hastened to form regiments of their own. The spectacle of unemployed workers making their way east via empty boxcars and an occasional stolen train was one of the most enduring images left by the depression of the 1890s. Courtesy Montana Historical Society, no.981-801.

144. The United States Army erected a special prison camp for members of the Coxey movement in a sagebrush wilderness along the Snake River in June 1894. The federal judge James H. Beatty chose the locale for reasons practical, symbolic, and perhaps even psychological. Located where the railroad crossed the river from Oregon, it was the one place most likely to deter more Coxeyites from heading east into Idaho. Their spirits crushed by the bleakness of confinement, many protesters sank into apathy and resignation. The movement faded from public consciousness after Coxey's arrest on Capitol Hill. Courtesy Idaho State Historical Society, no.247-z-2.

JUNE 1894

No.8 COXEY CAMP AT HUNTINGTON BRIDGE

145. The Frisco Mine in Gem, Idaho. This image dating from 1888 contains no hint that during the following decade two major episodes of industrial violence would wrack the Coeur d'Alene mining district, one in 1892 and one in 1899. The recurrent violence prompted a federal investigation of the area's labor relations, led to the assassination of the man who was governor during the second outbreak of violence, and culminated in the most famous trial in the history of the New Northwest, that of William D. Haywood and two associates for allegedly plotting to assassinate the former Idaho governor Frank Steunenberg. Courtesy Barnard-Stockbridge Collection, no.8-x134, University of Idaho Library.

FRISCO MILL AFTER EXPLOSION, JULY 11, 1892

146. The Frisco mill after the explosion of July 11, 1892. For several months, newly organized mineowners had confronted newly organized miners with a variety of antiunion weapons: they cut wages, hired spies and armed guards when workers struck, fired union members, and imported nonunion or scab labor. By mid-1892 the owners had employed more than eight hundred strikebreakers from outside the region and protected them with armed guards.

Months of escalating tension erupted in violence after the unmasking of "the cowboy detective," Charles A. Siringo, revealed the lengths to which mineowners were willing to go. Guards barricaded in the Frisco Mine's ore-processing mill in Gem exchanged gunshots with union members. Sporadic shooting continued for hours, then suddenly a roar shook the valley. Dynamiters had launched a bundle of explosives down a pipe that carried water into the mill. The blast demolished the structure, and falling timbers killed one worker and injured several others. The guards and scabs promptly surrendered, as did those at other mines and mills farther down the canyon. The violence left six men dead (three on each side) and about twenty-five injured. Courtesy Eastern Washington State Historical Society, no.L83-167.33

147. The 22d Infantry in Wallace, Idaho, in 1892. Following the Frisco explosion, Governor Norman B. Willey declared martial law. Some 1,300 federal troops joined the 192-man Idaho National Guard within days of the blast. Courtesy Barnard-Stockbridge Collection, no.8-x483, University of Idaho.

148. United States Army officers on duty in the Coeur d'Alene mining district in 1892. Soldiers rounded up hundreds of people and herded them into two makeshift prison camps, known as bull pens, at Wallace and Wardner, where many prisoners were confined for nearly two months awaiting a hearing. The state finally transported twenty-five union leaders to Boise for trial. Several of the accused used their time in the Ada County jail to create a new and more powerful union, the Western Federation of Miners. Courtesy Idaho State Historical Society, no. F 746.9.

149. Violence erupted once again in the Coeur d'Alene mining district in 1899, when a thousand striking miners took approximately three thousand pounds of dynamite from the Frisco Mine and used it to reduce the $250,000 Bunker Hill concentrator to a pile of rubble. Governor Frank Steunenberg declared martial law, and federal troops returned to the district. In this photograph they are encamped in Wallace. Courtesy Eastern Washington State Historical Society, no.L86-977.

150. Troops in 1899 again confined their prisoners to a makeshift prison, as they had in 1892. The bull pen was used because local jail facilities were too small to accommodate so many people. Of General Henry Clay Merriam's 528 prisoners in 1899, 330 were American citizens and 398 were single. Courtesy Barnard-Stockbridge Collection, no.8-x27, University of Idaho.

Conditions Will Soon Become Intolerable

Wardner, May 11, 1899

Governor Steunenberg, Boise, Idaho:

I am still holding nearly 500 prisoners in a barn and box cars. All are very uncomfortable and with unsanitary conditions which will soon become intolerable. Something must be done to hurry preliminary examination and release of those not prima facie guilty. It is impracticable to make this large number of prisoners reasonably comfortable here without considerable time and expense. Can you not personally inspect the situation here and bring help?

Merriam, Brigadier-General

– "Coeur D'Alene Mining Troubles," 56th Cong., 1st Sess., 1899, Senate Document 142 p.34

151. Labor militancy: prisoners drilling inside the bull pen on April 29, 1899. "Every union," advised Ed Boyce, president of the Western Federation of Miners, "should have a rifle club." The photograph conveys the warlike atmosphere that prevailed in various mining regions of the northern Rocky Mountains at the turn of the century. Courtesy Barnard-Stockbridge Collection, no. 8-x3 1 2, University of Idaho.

52. A bloody postscript to the Coeur d'Alene mining wars occurred in Caldwell, Idaho, where on December 30, 1905, an explosion triggered by opening the front gate to his home killed the former governor Frank Steunenberg. Courtesy Idaho State Historical Society, no.71-84.2.

153. Frank Steunenberg, who had once been a member of a printers' union, was a man who liked to emphasize the common touch: he refused to wear a necktie to any state function. With the backing of organized labor he was elected governor in 1896 and again in 1898, but he could not condone violence in the Coeur d'Alenes. Courtesy Idaho State Historical Society, no.13.

154. Harry Orchard, the man who killed Steunenberg and wrote a bloody postscript to the Coeur d'Alene violence. For this crime, the state convicted and sentenced Orchard to spend the rest of his life in prison. He cheated the gallows only by claiming that top officials of the Western Federation of Miners had actually hired him to assassinate the former governor in revenge for his actions in the Coeur d'Alene dispute six years earlier. Courtesy Idaho State Historical Society, no.72-64.1.

155. Armed with Orchard's long and sordid confession, Idaho officials quietly pursued William D. ("Big Bill") Haywood, the WFM's secretary-treasurer; Charles Moyer, its president; and George Pettibone, a blacklisted Coeur d'Alene miner turned hardware merchant. With the full support of the governor of Colorado, Idaho lawmen kidnapped the three suspects in Denver and rushed them to Boise on a special train. The extradition by abduction outraged organized labor and civil libertarians and focused national attention on the case. Pictured here from left to right are Pettibone, Haywood, and Moyer awaiting trial in 1907. The dramatic case pitted Idaho's special prosecutor and newly elected United States senator, William E. Borah, against the famed Chicago attorney Clarence Darrow for the defense. For almost two months, the proceedings dominated local and national news. In the end a jury deliberated twenty hours before acquitting Haywood. After another jury acquitted Pettibone, the state dropped all charges against Moyer. Courtesy Idaho State Historical Society, no. 2004.

156. Not all violence was between labor and management. Some of it involved factional disputes within local labor organizations, as was the case in Butte, when a dissident group of miners worked through the night of June 23, 1914, to destroy the Miners Union Hall. After each of twenty-six blasts, they fired revolvers into the air to warn back the crowd of onlookers. Meanwhile, policemen played cards at their headquarters rather than intervene. Courtesy Montana Historical Society, no. 946-112.

157. Four victims of the Everett Massacre appeared on a postcard distributed by Wobblies to raise funds. The reverse side reads, "DIED FOR FREE SPEECH – THE EVERETT MASSACRE – Bloody Sunday, November 5, 1916." Courtesy Special Collections Division, University of Washington Libraries, UW no. 1537.

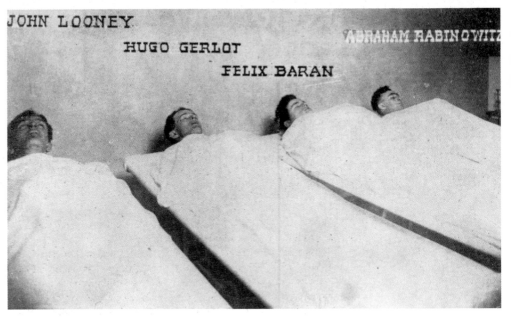

158. Darius Kinsey photographed this contingent of the Spruce Production Division. The years before and during World War I in one Washington lumber center, Raymond, were recalled in the state's WPA guide: "The depressed conditions resulted also in unemployment and economic distress. During this troubled time, members of the I. W. W. were driven from the city by a vigilante 'pick-handle brigade.' By 1915, however, prosperity returned, and the expansion of the lumber market resulted in the enlargement of the lumber plants; at the same time a branch of the Chicago, Milwaukee, St. Paul and Pacific Railroad was completed, making new markets accessible to the wood-products industry. Many new logging camps were opened up; and during the First World War ten wooden freighters were launched from a hastily built shipyard. Controversy between lumber operators and workers over hours, wages, and conditions threatened to curtail production at a time when lumber was acutely needed. After several companies of the United States Army's Spruce Division had been stationed in Raymond, the crisis passed. Working conditions were considerably improved, and several sawmills began to operate. The town's population soared to nearly 7,000." *Washington, A Guide to the Evergreen State* (1941), 562. Courtesy D. Kinsey Collection, no.18431, Whatcom Museum of History and Art.

159. The strike in the Skinner and Eddy shipyards, January 21, 1919, was a prelude to the Seattle General Strike. This four-day work stoppage in February 1919 was neither violent nor revolutionary, but because it was the first major general strike in American history and occurred shortly after the Soviets took power in Russia, it frightened many people. The strike originated with a complaint by Seattle's numerous shipyard workers that their wages had failed to keep pace with the inflation caused by World War I. Their plight attracted the sympathy of others and culminated in the general strike by sixty thousand Seattle workers. Mayor Ole Hanson, who did much to foster the impression that he had contained a revolutionary outbreak, resigned his office for the lecture circuit, spinning an incredible tale of subversive plots that he published as *Bolshevism versus Americanism* (Garden City, NY: Doubleday, Page & Co., 1920). Courtesy Washington State Historical Society, A. Curtis no.37055.

160. Wobblies in 1936 struck the logging camps around Saint Maries, Idaho, to press their demand for higher wages. In one incident, company-hired plug-uglies opened fire on pickets, severely wounding several of them. A court later fined ten of the company men $500 each, and the state declared martial law in the face of rising tensions. Wobblies distributed this picture of one victim in an effort to raise money. Courtesy Idaho State Historical Society, no.73-124.2.

Subversive Words: No One Knows Where

Two days before the [Seattle General] strike I wrote:

We are undertaking the most tremendous move ever made by labor in this country, a move that will lead – No One Knows where! We do not need hysteria! We need the iron march of labor.

Labor will feed the people . . .

Labor will care for the babies and the sick . . .

Labor will preserve order . . .

Not the withdrawal of labor power, but the power of workers to manage, will win this strike. . . . The closing down of our industries as a mere shut-down will not affect those eastern gentlemen much. But the closing down of the capitalistically-owned industries of Seattle while the workers organize to feed the people, care for babies and maintain order – this will move them, for this looks too much like the taking of power by workers. . . .

If the strike continues, labor may feel led to open more and more activities under its own management.

That is why I say that we are starting on a road that leads – NO ONE KNOWS WHERE!

This editorial quoted from coast to coast as an official expression, was hailed by our local progressives as the "first constructive explanation." "You have shown us something to gain from this strike – education in management." But did sixty thousand workers strike for education? Later when I was arrested, this editorial was one of the counts against me. Its very vagueness saved me. "No one knows where"—the prosecution claimed this threatened anarchy. The defense retorted that it merely admitted the fact that the future is unknown. Neither gave the real essence of those words. They appealed to the faith of the pioneer in inevitable progress; they stirred the passion of the march to the undiscovered West. – Anna Louise Strong, *I Change Worlds* (New York: H. Holt, 1935), 79

Beyond the Wageworkers' Frontier

The decline of the IWW as an organization kept pace with the diminishing role of the floating workers in the West through the introduction of farm machinery, the completion of the building of the railroads, the tendency of the workers to "settle down" in the lumber industry, etc. – William Z. Foster, *Pages from a Worker's Life* (1939)

When news of the Cat Creek [Montana] discovery was flashed over the West, a mad stampede, resembling an old-time gold rush, occurred. Oil prospectors, however, reached their destination more swiftly and with less hardship than the pilgrims who came with pick and pan 50 years earlier. Every type of car was pressed into service; expensive limousines stirred the dust of old cattle trails beside wheezing models that wobbled along on warped wheels. – *Montana, A State Guide Book* (1939)

In Montana's "wide, open spaces" the cowpuncher no longer rides hour after hour, unimpeded by fences. He wears few fancy togs and carries no gun; he is a workingman who does his job well and cares nothing about the traditions of the motion-picture West. – *Montana, A State Guide Book* (1939)

Progress has impoverished the skidroad, and in these days it is a dull and dismal section in any of the cities named [Vancouver, Seattle, Tacoma, Portland, and the smaller lumber towns]. The logger no longer "blows" all of his earnings in the skidroad hangouts. He very often drives a car when he comes to town at a shutdown; he wears royal raiment that makes him presentable as anybody in any crowd; so he stops at a first-class hotel, attends the theater, eats in tony restaurants and cafeterias, and he hotfoots it with nice city girls in the best jazz palaces.

I am speaking of the typical young logger, of course, the one who didn't know the camps before they had modern living conditions, big wages, and jobs calling for highly skilled labor; the young logger who never knew the skidroad in the days of its prosperity and glory. He only knows the skidroad now when his cash runs low and he is compelled to stand before the blackboards, waiting for a job to be chalked up.

The old-time loggers still stick to the skidroad. It was their home place in the old days, and they find it hard to change. If they have to come to town to get their teeth fixed or to have their rheumatism treated, the bootlegger is always handy there. If a crowd of them come in because of one of the periodical shutdowns, there are soft-drink bars that retain a faint gleam from the light, and a frail scent from the odors of the roaring, glittering, smelly old-time skidroad saloon. The old gambling houses are gone, but there are still rummy parlors on the skidroad. The dance halls are gone, but the mechanical piano tinkles and clangs in Wild West and White Slave movie theaters. The "coffee and" joints and the cheap rooming houses are little changed. Dull and dismal though it now is, the skidroad is still home to the old-time logger when he is in town. – James Stevens, "Skidroad Palaces" (1927)

The Pacific Limited enters Oregon from the east in the morning and has crossed the State by nightfall, and occasionally a traveler sits at the window of the swaying observation car and wonders at the incongruity of all this. From the break of day the train clatters for hours over sections that could grow millions of bushels of wheat and graze thousands of herds of cattle. The afternoon sees it crashing past dense stands of prime timber. As the sun begins to dip behind the hills, the big locomotive enters the river gorge where billions of kilowatt-hours of electricity are as undeveloped as if Franklin had never sent his kite into the thunderheads. On the last mile of this journey, a few hundred yards from the station at Portland, the train rolls through Sullivan's Gulch. The gulch is spanned by a viaduct with heavy steel pillars set in concrete foundations. Built against these bases are scores of shanties made from laths and tar-paper and discarded lumber. Fires flicker in the evening dusk, and over them men are cooking dinner in battered ten-pound tomato cans. The men are dirty and ragged. Their clothes are not made from the wool of the countless sheep that could graze on the hills the train passed in the morning. They are not eating the grain that might be grown on the uncultivated plains the train whizzed past at midday. They are not housed in homes that could be built from the millions of board-feet of timber the Limited roared by in the late afternoon. They do not enjoy the benefit of the latent electric energy the travelers saw in the Columbia River at twilight.

This is life in a hundred shanty towns, in the nation's richest vault of natural resources, in the year 1938. – Richard L. Neuberger, *Our Promised Land* (1938)

161. An image from Montana's Cat
Creek oil field in the 1920s. The
first significant discovery of oil in
the state dated from 1915, and was
followed by a series of oil booms
that seemed to signify a new post-
war era defined by internal combus-
tion engines and automobile
transportation. Courtesy Montana
Historical Society, no.973-252.

62. Construction workers used hand tools to extend the Great Northern Railway across Montana Territory near Fort Belknap in 1887. Courtesy Montana Historical Society.

63. Thirty years later: a steam shovel used in construction of the Spokane & Inland Empire Railroad north of Moscow, Idaho, exemplified the displacement of hand labor and underscored the role that technology played in ending the wageworkers' frontier. Courtesy Eastern Washington State Historical Society, no.8708.

164. Teamsters photographed in Boise, Idaho, around the turn of the century. The majority of such workers operated only locally, hauling freight to and from the railroad depot and forming part of a network of distribution within the city. Railroads dominated intercity transportation until the 1920s in all but the most remote corners of the region. Courtesy Idaho State Historical Society, no.3 73-150.2.

165. The Pacific Northwest labor leader Dave Beck benefited from the growth of the intercity trucking industry in the 1930s and 1940s. Expansion of this industry in the years following the close of the old wageworkers' frontier offered labor a new field for organization. Beck moved rapidly through the ranks of the Teamsters' Union – from organizing laundry drivers in Seattle to being elected national head of the union (1952–62). In the mid-1930s, he was easily the Teamsters' most powerful regional leader and the dominant personality in Northwest labor. Courtesy Special Collections Division, University of Washington Libraries, UW no.860.

166. Seattle's Hooverville, a community of shacks fashioned from tarpaper and tin and packing crates, sprawled across the city's tideflats during the depression decade of the 1930s. A sociologist who studied the community was startled to find one resident bedded down in a coffin. Most of the inhabitants were homeless men, many of whom had once worked as the loggers, fishermen, hard-rock miners, bridge carpenters, sewer diggers, and others who exemplified the wageworkers' frontier. This Hooverville was photographed from the Skinner and Eddy shipyards on June 10, 1937. In Portland a similar shantytown developed in Sullivan's Gulch. Courtesy Special Collections Division, University of Washington Libraries, Lee no. 20102.

167. Thousands of Seattle's unemployed gathered on June 6, 1932, to pressure John F. (Johnny) Dore, who was elected mayor that year, to relieve their plight. Colorful and popular, Dore sought to distinguish himself as a friend of workers, especially of Dave Beck's Teamsters. Ironically, he had entered public office with a reputation as an anti-labor reactionary, but following defeat in 1934, he was relected mayor two years later with the help of the Teamsters he had once implied were racketeers and terrorists. Courtesy Special Collections Division, University of Washington Libraries, Lee no.20121.

168. Collecting funds for the Bonus
Army in Portland, 1932. This
movement originated in the Oregon metropolis in May and sought
to pressure Congress into giving
needy World War I veterans a promised bonus immediately instead of
forcing them to wait until 1946. As
the main contingent of the Bonus

Expeditionary Force headed east in
boxcars and ancient automobiles, it
gathered supporters along the way.
Twenty-five thousand members
reached Washington, DC, where
they established a shantytown on
the flats of the Anacostia River to
await legislative action. Congress
rejected their demands, and the

United States Army routed them in
late July with saber, bayonet, and
tear gas. The Bonus Army recalled
the unemployment protest of Jacob
Coxey's legions in 1894 and perhaps even some of the unorthodox
tactics of the Industrial Workers of
the World. Courtesy Oregon Historical Society, no.CN 009027.

69. A migrant family traveling by freight train, Toppenish, Yakima Valley, August 1939. "During the annual harvest, the routine of the city [Yakima] is interrupted by an influx of migratory workers and their families. At the height of the season in September, approximately 35,000 agricultural workers are required full-time in the fields and orchards, in contrast to late fall and spring, when only about 500 are needed. The migratory family solves the problem of seasonal labor for Yakima Valley agriculture; but it raises another problem, for its annual income is seldom sufficient to sustain it during periods of unemployment between harvests.

"Wearing straw or old felt hats, blue denim shirts, jeans, cotton dresses, or slacks, these migratory workers arrive just before the active season begins. Shortly, lodging houses and camps are filled; tent camps are set up along irrigation ditches and at the edges of orchards; streets are crowded with job seekers. During free time they seek recreation in movies or beer parlors, or throng the sidewalks, window-shopping along the streets where many stores keep open to catch late business." – *Washington, A Guide to the Evergreen State* (Portland: Binfords & Mort, 1941), 300. Courtesy Library of Congress, no.LC-USF34-20314.

170. A migratory family seeking
work harvesting potatoes in
Klamath County, Oregon. Courtesy Library of Congress,
no.LC-USF34-21974-C.

Heading West to the Promised Land

It is no romantic fiction that Middle Westerners dispossessed by the drought are invad-
ing the sundown seaboard. Felix Belair,
covering the dust storms and heat spells for
the New York *Times,* wrote, "Farmers with
their possessions and families loaded into
trucks that normally would be carrying a second crop of hay were headed west to Oregon,
Washington, and Idaho." – Richard L. Neuberger, *Our Promised Land* (New York: Macmillan, 1938), 34

171. Migrants in search of a "promised land" confronted this sign, erected by the state's Department of Public Assistance, at Idaho's eastern boundary. Courtesy Library of Congress, no. LC-USF34-65540-D.

Idaho, We're Busted Flat

With increasing frequency we heard the Pacific Northwest mentioned as a haven for the Dust Bowl refugee. A World War veteran used his bonus money to take his family to Northern Idaho. He wrote back accounts of cheap, cutover land, of abundant rains and beautiful gardens.

The peak of migration to the Pacific Northwest was reached in 1936. We heard of no migrants coming back, or going elsewhere, once they had reached "the promised land." . . . We chose the north end of the Panhandle of Idaho because it offered cheap land, good soil, and abundant moisture. Except for the fact that we would be among strangers, we could be no worse off in this strange land than in our own, and it was imperative that we take the children out of the dust. . . .

For six days we coaxed the weary, heavy-laden old car along, westward and northward. As mile after mile passed, certain other equipages became familiar to us. Here was an old truck with a Colorado license plate. Under a "tarp" stretched across the back was an assortment of children, luggage, and household goods. Across one open side flapped a piece of heavy cardboard on which was scrawled:

> Idaho, we're busted flat.
> Here we come in spite of that;
> Not expecting wealth or gain —
> Just want our kids to see it rain.

If we passed this outfit during the forenoon, it usually passed us before evening. Twice, when night overtook us, we stopped at the same cabin court. We have wondered about this family many times since. Did they find the land of their dreams? – Nelle Portrey Davis, *Stump Ranch Pioneer* (New York: Dodd, Mead, 1942), 38–39

A Land of Opportunity

At the start of construction for the Bonneville and Grand Coulee dams, President Franklin D. Roosevelt had called national attention to the Pacific Northwest as a promised land in a speech that contained these stirring words:

In this Northwestern section of the land, we still have an opportunity for a vastly increased population. There are many sections of the country, as you know, where conditions are crowded. There are many sections of the country where land has run out or been put to the wrong kind of use. America is growing. There are many people who want to go to a section of the country where they will have a better chance for themselves and their children — and there are a great many people who have children and need room for growing families. Out here you have not just space, you have space that can be used by human beings — a wonderful land — a land of opportunity. — Quoted in Richard L. Neuberger, *Our Promised Land* (New York: Macmillan, 1938), 44

172. "Oregon or Bust." Arthur Rothstein photographed Vernon Evans near Missoula, Montana, in July 1936. He left Lemmon, South Dakota, in search of a better life in Oregon or Washington. Courtesy Library of Congress, no. LC-USF34-5008-D.

173. In this 1934 photograph, an Oregon highway patrolman directs a job seeker to the construction site of the Bonneville Dam. Courtesy National Archives, no.69-N-P-1004.

174. Bonneville Dam under construction. Franklin D. Roosevelt promised in his 1932 presidential campaign to undertake hydroelectric development on the Columbia River. Construction of Bonneville and Grand Coulee dams was well suited to the New Deal's goal of relieving widespread unemployment. Courtesy Oregon Historical Society, no.79632.

175. The boomtown of Grand Coulee, Washington, in October 1934. Richard Neuberger, journalist and later United States senator from Oregon, described this brief re-creation of the wageworkers' frontier: "Grand Coulee – as well as the other towns which merge with it – sprawls over the uplands above the great dam like a torn and ragged carpet. There is no order or planning. Shacks and cabins dot the hills as unevenly as marbles rolled on a rug. The streets are rut-strewn and sloping. In wet weather they are a series of ponds, and in dry weather they are prolific manufacturers of dust. If the gasoline pumps were hitching posts and the neon signs were oil lamps, Grand Coulee might be one of the mushroom towns which followed the Northern Pacific westward." – *Our Promised Land* (New York: Macmillan, 1938), 373. Courtesy Eastern Washington State Historical Society, no. L87-1.4650-34.

176. Franklin D. Roosevelt at Grand Coulee Dam in August 1934. A few days earlier the president had arrived in Portland from Hawaii aboard the cruiser USS *Houston*. Approximately 150,000 people turned out to greet him in a parade, which was followed by a trip to Bonneville Dam. There workers gave him a whistle-blowing, steam shovel salute. Continuing north to the proposed site of Grand Coulee Dam, the president addressed a crowd of 25,000 listeners. Roosevelt returned to dedicate Bonneville Dam in September 1937 and to inspect progress at Grand Coulee Dam. Courtesy Eastern Washington State Historical Society, no.L87-1.4350-34.

177. Construction workers at Grand Coulee Dam in 1938. Seven thousand men from all over the Pacific Northwest worked on this gigantic construction project in a remote part of Washington. "Every element – good, bad, and indifferent – that goes to compose a community in the hinterlands, joined the parade. Over the desertlike plateau of the Columbia a veritable caravan rolled. From trucks, wagons, and trailers protruded barber chairs, hand printing presses, and permanent-waving machines. Cooks dreamed of making fortunes out of hamburgers and custard pie and beer. Real-estate agents visioned lucrative returns on the quick turnover of lots and sections. Ministers thought of men to reform spiritually and morally. Prostitutes imagined ready dollars." – Richard Neuberger, *Our Promised Land*, (New York: Macmillan, 1938), 374. Courtesy Eastern Washington State Historical Society, no.1295.

178. Grand Coulee Dam in 1942 was so immense a structure that journalists struggled to find words to describe its size. "Four ocean liners the size of the giant *Queen Mary* could be placed on the crest of the dam, and still they would not stretch from one end to the other. In bulk Grand Coulee will exceed the twenty next largest dams in the country combined. It will contain enough concrete to build a standard automobile highway from Philadelphia to Seattle and back by way of Los Angeles. Sufficient water will flow through the dam each year to provide New York City's drinking supply for a century. In the twin powerhouses, each more than twice as high as the Leaning Tower of Pisa, so much electricity will be generated that all the switches will have to be thrown far away from the plant by remote control; otherwise the men operating the dam would be instantly electrocuted," explained Richard Neuberger in the mid-1930s.

"A surprising feature is the preponderant number of young men employed at Grand Coulee. Waiting in line to eat in the mess hall, I noticed dozens of tall lads wearing football sweaters from near-by colleges and universities. The work is dangerous and scarcely a day passes without some one's being injured; fifty-four men have already been killed. I talked with some of the older men engaged in specialized tasks, and discovered that a considerable portion of them had drifted to Coulee after completion of the giant Boulder Dam on the Colorado River." – *Our Promised Land* (New York: Macmillan, 1938), 69–70, 73. Courtesy Library of Congress, no. 11604-262-91300.

179. Less spectacular than Bonneville and Grand Coulee dams but no less important to the region's jobless were the myriad projects funded by the Works Progress Administration, like improving the streets of Seattle in 1936 or writing guides to each of the states. Courtesy Washington State Historical Society, no. WPA 3570.

180. Another boon to the jobless was forest-fire training at the Skagit Camp of the Civilian Conservation Corps, seen here on September 16, 1933. The CCC put young men to work on reforestation projects. In Idaho, where it employed eighteen thousand men and left a lasting impression on the state's landscape, it was probably the most popular New Deal agency. Courtesy Forest Service Photographic Collection, National Agricultural Library, no. 16700.

181. World War II brought prosperity after a decade of depression. High wages created an unreal situation for many people who had weathered hard times during the 1930s. Even before a formal declaration of war in December 1941, the Pacific Northwest experienced the impact of increased production for defense and for aid to friendly nations already at war. The region's best-known war industries were the Kaiser shipyards in the Portland-Vancouver area and Boeing Aircraft, with large assembly plants in Seattle and Renton. With the aid of federal subsidies, the industrialist Henry J. Kaiser became the world's foremost shipbuilder and for a time employed nearly 100,000 people in his yards, displacing Pacific Telephone and Telegraph as Portland's largest employer. This was 70 percent of the city's total war labor force. This photograph is of quitting time in October 1944 at the Oregon Shipbuilding Corporation. Courtesy Oregon Historical Society, no.006452.

182. Preparing to attach a heavy deckhouse to the hull of a Liberty ship under construction at the Oregon Shipbuilding Corporation, a joint venture of Henry J. Kaiser's construction empire and Todd Shipyards. Between mid-1941, when his first yard opened on the banks of the Willamette River, until August 1945, various Kaiser enterprises constructed some fifty small aircraft carriers and several hundred merchant Liberty ships using fast and simplified methods of welding. New workers seeking good jobs in Portland arrived from ranches in Idaho and Montana, even as far away as New York City, in special trains chartered by Kaiser. Courtesy Oregon Historical Society, no.87181.

183. The "Grandma Crew" at Oregon Shipbuilding Corporation contained six grandmothers out of a total of eight production workers. Courtesy Oregon Historical Society, no.006451.

184. Wheeling out the final B-17 Flying Fortress built in Seattle. It is decorated with the names of missions flown by B-17s. In addition to the nearly 7,000 B-17s produced in Seattle, Boeing also rolled out a total of 1,119 B-29s. Employment jumped from approximately four thousand in 1939 to nearly fifty-five thousand in 1944. Courtesy Oregon Historical Society, no.CN 004871.

185. Women assembling part of a
B-29 at Boeing. At the peak of wartime production in 1944, approximately 46 percent of the aircraft
builder's employees were women.
In the Puget Sound Naval Shipyard, employment of women in
production jobs increased from virtually none in 1941 to 21 percent of
the yard's thirty thousand employees in mid-1943. In all the important industrial facilities of the
Puget Sound area combined,
women formed about one-fourth of
the work force. Courtesy the Boeing Company Archives.

186. Workers using an electric saw to fell timber in the Malheur National Forest in August 1943. An inadequate number of houses built during the war coupled with an increase in the number of new families – especially the latter – kept the Northwest's forest products industry producing at record levels for more than two decades after the war, though at the cost of reducing the region's timber supply. Courtesy Forest Service Photographic Collection, National Agricultural Library, no.426966.

187. Soldiers in the Arsenal of Democracy. Quitting time at Anaconda's copper smelter in Montana in September 1942. Courtesy Library of Congress, no.LC-USW3-8625-D.

188. A welder at Oregon Shipbuilding Corporation in 1942. When the war ended three years later, one contemporary observed that many female workers were "retiring to their homes." Unlike their World War I predecessors, many of these wage-earning women would return to the industrial work force. The shrinking ranks of itinerant single males and the permanent addition of women to the ranks of industrial workers were two key trends that clearly distinguished labor in the modern Pacific Northwest from that of the old wageworkers' frontier. Courtesy Oregon Historical Society, no. 56117.

For Further Reading

Selected Publications on Labor & the Work Environment in the New Northwest

Bercuson, David Jay. "Labour Radicalism and the Western Industrial Frontier." *Canadian Historical Review* 58 (1977): 154–75.

Berner, Richard C. *Seattle, 1921–1940: From Boom to Bust.* Seattle: Charles Press, 1992. This book contains some excellent chapters on labor.

Brown, Ronald C. *Hard-Rock Miners: The Intermountain West, 1860–1920.* College Station: Texas A&M University Press, 1979.

Broyles, Glen J. "The Spokane Free Speech Fight, 1909–1910: A Study in IWW Tactics." *Labor History* 19 (1978): 238–52.

Calvert, Jerry W. *The Gibraltar: Socialism and Labor in Butte, Montana, 1895–1920.* Helena: Montana Historical Society Press, 1988.

Campbell, Robert A. "Blacks and the Coal Mines of Western Washington, 1888–1896." *Pacific Northwest Quarterly* 73 (1982): 146–55.

Clark, Norman H. *Mill Town: A Social History of Everett, Washington, from Its Earliest Beginnings on the Shores of Puget Sound to the Tragic and Infamous Event Known as the Everett Massacre.* Seattle: University of Washington Press, 1970.

Conlin, Joseph R. "The IWW and the Question of Violence." *Wisconsin Magazine of History* 51 (1968): 316–18.

———. "Old Boy, Did You Get Enough Pie?" *Journal of Forest History* 23 (1979): 165–85. Life in logging camps.

Copeland, Tom. "Wesley Everest, IWW Martyr." *Pacific Northwest Quarterly* 77 (1986): 122–29.

Daniel, Cletus E. "Wobblies on the Farm: The IWW in the Yakima Valley." *Pacific Northwest Quarterly* 65 (1974): 166–75.

Dembo, John. *An Historical Bibliography of Washington State Labor and Laboring Classes.* Seattle: J. Dembo, 1978.

———. *Unions and Politics in Washington State, 1885–1935.* New York: Garland Publishing, 1983.

Derickson, Alan. *Workers' Health, Workers' Democracy: The Western Miners' Struggle, 1891–1925.* Ithaca: Cornell University Press, 1988.

Dubofsky, Melvyn. *We Shall Be All: A History of the Industrial Workers of the World.* Chicago: Quadrangle, 1969.

Emmons, David M. *The Butte Irish: Class and Ethnicity in an American Mining Town, 1875–1925.* Urbana: University of Illinois Press, 1989.

Fahey, John. *The Days of the Hercules.* Moscow: University Press of Idaho, 1978.

Ficken, Robert E. "The Wobbly Horrors: Pacific Northwest Lumbermen and the Industrial Workers of the World, 1917–1928." *Labor History* 24 (1983): 326–65.

Flaherty, Stacy A. "Boycott in Butte: Organized Labor and the Chinese Community, 1896–1897." *Montana, the Magazine of Western History* 37 (Winter 1987): 34–47.

Foster, Jim. "The Ten Day Tramps." *Labor History* 23 (1982): 608–23.

Friedheim, Robert L. *The Seattle General Strike.* Seattle: University of Washington Press, 1964.

Gamboa, Erasmo. *Mexican Labor and World War II: Braceros in the Pacific Northwest, 1942–1947.* Austin: University of Texas Press, 1990.

Grover, David H. *Debaters and Dynamiters: The Story of the Haywood Trial.* Corvallis: Oregon State University Press, 1964.

Gutfeld, Arnon. "The Murder of Frank Little: Radical Labor Agitation in Butte, Montana, 1917." *Labor History* 10 (1969): 177–92.

———. "The Speculator Disaster in 1917: Labor Resurgence at Butte, Montana." *Arizona and the West* 11 (Spring 1969): 27–38.

Hallberg, Gerald N. "Bellingham, Washington's Anti-Hindu Riot." *Journal of the West* 12 (1973): 163–75.

Hart, Patricia, and Ivar Nelson. *Mining Town: The Photographic Record of T. N. Barnard and Nellie Stockbridge from the Coeur d'Alenes.* Seattle: University of Washington Press, 1984.

Hynding, Alan A. "The Coal Miners of Washington Territory: Labor Troubles in 1888–89." *Arizona and the West* 12 (1970): 221–36.

Ichioka, Yugi. "Japanese Immigrant Labor Contractors and the Northern Pacific and Great Northern Railroad Companies, 1898–1907." *Labor History* 21 (1980): 325–50.

Jensen, Vernon. *Lumber and Labor.* New York: Farrar & Rinehart, 1945.

———. *Heritage of Conflict: Labor Relations in the Nonferrous Metals Industry up to 1930.* Ithaca: Cornell University Press, 1950.

Karlin, Jules A. "The Anti-Chinese Outbreaks in Seattle, 1885, 1886." *Pacific Northwest Quarterly* 39 (1948): 103–30.

———. "The Anti-Chinese Outbreak in Tacoma, 1885." *Pacific Historical Review* 27 (August 1954): 271–83.

Laurie, Clayton D. "'The Chinese Must Go': The United States Army and the Anti-Chinese Riots in Washington Territory, 1885–1886." *Pacific Northwest Quarterly* 81 (1990): 22–29.

Lembcke, Jerry, and William M. Tattam. *One Union in Wood: A Political History of the International Woodworkers of America.* New York: International Publishers, 1984.

LeWarne, Charles Pierce. *Utopias on Puget Sound, 1885–1915.* Seattle: University of Washington Press, 1975.

Lingenfelter, Richard E. *The Hardrock Miners: A History of the Mining Labor Movement in the American West, 1863–1893.* Berkeley: University of California Press, 1974.

Lovin, Hugh T. "Moses Alexander and the Idaho Lumber Strike of 1917: The Wartime Ordeal of a Progressive." *Pacific Northwest Quarterly* 66 (1975): 115–22.

McClelland, John M., Jr. *Wobbly War: The Centralia Story.* Tacoma: Washington State Historical Society, 1987.

McGregor, Alexander Campbell. *Counting Sheep: From Open Range to Agribusiness on the Columbia Plateau.* Seattle: University of Washington Press, 1982.

McWilliams, Carey, *Ill Fares the Land: Migrants and Migratory Labor in the United States.* Boston: Little, Brown and Company, 1942.

Malone, Michael. *The Battle for Butte: Mining and Politics on the Northern Frontier, 1864–1906.* Seattle: University of Washington Press, 1981.

Monkkonen, Eric H., ed. *Walking to Work: Tramps in America, 1790–1935.* Lincoln: University of Nebraska Press, 1984.

Nelson, Bruce. *Workers on the Waterfront: Seamen, Longshoremen, and Unionism in the 1930s.* Urbana: University of Illinois Press, 1988.

Newbill, James G. "Farmers and Wobblies in the Yakima Valley, 1933." *Pacific Northwest Quarterly* 68 (1977): 80–87.

O'Connor, Harvey. *Revolution in Seattle: A Memoir.* 1964. Reprint. Seattle: Left Bank Books, 1981.

Parker, Carleton. *The Casual Laborer and Other Essays.* New York: Harcourt, Brace and Howe, 1920.

Petersen, Keith C. *Potlatch, Idaho, and the Potlatch Lumber Company.* Pullman: Washington State University Press, 1987.

Peterson, Richard H. "Conflict and Consensus: Labor Relations in Western Mining." *Journal of the West* 12 (January 1973): 1–17.

Phipps, Stanley S. *From Bull Pen to Bargaining Table: The Tumultuous Struggle of the Coeur D'Alenes Miners for the Right to Organize, 1887–1942.* New York: Garland Publishing, 1988.

Prouty, Andrew Mason. *More Deadly than War: Pacific Coast Logging, 1827–1981.* New York: Garland Publishing, 1985.

Rajala, Richard A. "Bill and the Boss: Protest, Technological Change, and the Transformation of the West Coast Logging Camp, 1890–1930." *Journal of Forest History* 33 (1989): 168–79.

Robbins, William G. *Hard Times in Paradise: Coos Bay, Oregon.* Seattle: University of Washington Press, 1988.

Rohe, Randall E. "After the Gold Rush: Chinese Mining in the Far West, 1850–1900." *Montana, the Magazine of Western History* 32 (Autumn 1982): 2–19.

Schwantes, Carlos A. *Radical Heritage: Labor, Socialism, and Reform in Washington and British Columbia, 1885–1917.* Seattle: University of Washington Press, 1979.

Shovers, Brian. "The Perils of Working in the Butte Underground: Industrial Fatalities in the Copper Mines, 1880–1920." *Montana, the Magazine of Western History* 37 (Spring 1987): 26–39.

Skold, Karen Beck. "The Job He Left Behind: Women in the Shipyards during World War II." In *Women in Pacific Northwest History: An Anthology,* edited by Karen J. Blair, 107–29. Seattle: University of Washington Press, 1988.

Smith, Robert W. *The Coeur d'Alene Mining War: A Case Study of an Industrial Dispute.* Corvallis: Oregon State University Press, 1961.

Sonneman, Toby F. *Fruit Fields in My Blood:*

Okie Migrants in the West. Moscow: University of Idaho Press, 1992.

Spence, Clark C. "Knights of the Tie and Rail – Tramps and Hoboes in the West." *Western Historical Quarterly* 2 (1971): 5–19.

Stegner, S. Page. "Protest Songs from the Butte Miners." *Western Folklore* 26 (April 1967): 157–67.

Stern Mark. "Black Strikebreakers in the Coal Fields: King County, Washington – 1891." *Journal of Ethnic Studies* 5 (Fall 1977): 60–70.

Stone, Harry W. "Beginning of Labor Movement in the Pacific Northwest." *Oregon Historical Quarterly* 47 (1946): 155–64.

Tyler, Robert L. *Rebels of the Woods: The I.W.W. in the Pacific Northwest.* Eugene: University of Oregon Press, 1967.

———. "The United States Government as Union Organizer: The Loyal Legion of Loggers and Lumbermen." *Mississippi Valley Historical Review* 47 (1960): 434–51.

Wells, Merle W. "Twentieth-Century Migrant Farm Labor." *Journal of the West* 25 (April 1986): 65–72.

White, W. Thomas. "Railroad Labor Protests, 1894–1917: From Community to Class in the Pacific Northwest." *Pacific Northwest Quarterly* 75 (1984): 13–21.

Williams, William J. "Bloody Sunday Revisited." *Pacific Northwest Quarterly* 71 (1980): 50–62. An eyewitness account of the Everett massacre.

Wyman, Mark. *Hard Rock Epic: Western Miners and the Industrial Revolution, 1860–1890.* Berkeley: University of California Press, 1979.

Wynne, Robert E. "American Labor Leaders and the Vancouver Anti-Oriental Riot." *Pacific Northwest Quarterly* 57 (1966): 172–79.

Zellick, Anna. "Fire in the Hole: Slovenians, Croatians, and Coal Mining on the Musselshell." *Montana, the Magazine of Western History* 40 (Spring 1990): 16–31.

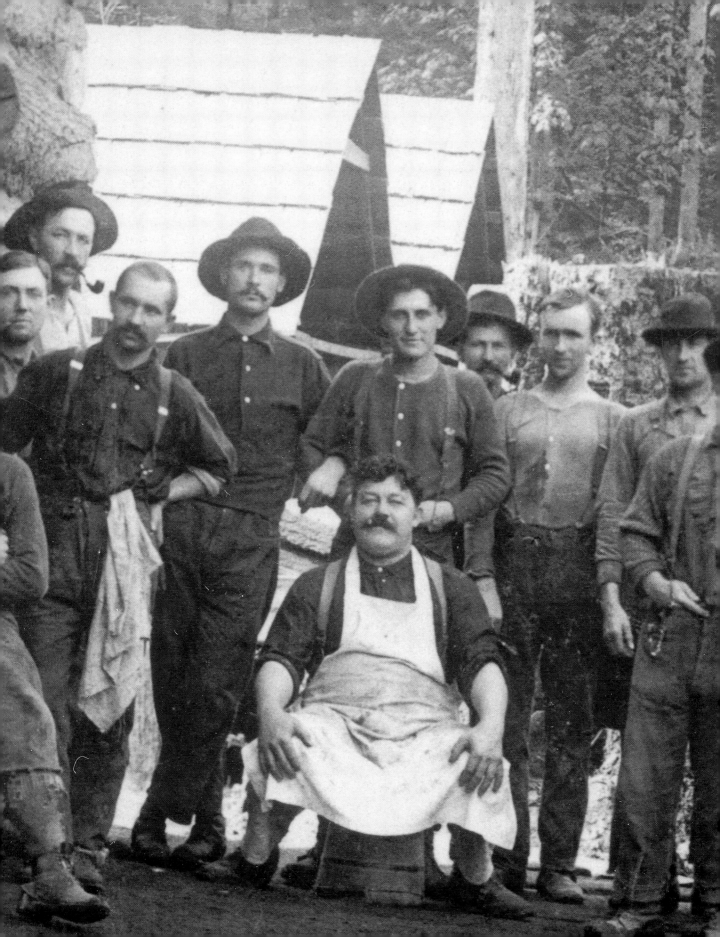

Index